TO JACK AND LAKEESHA
NEW FRIENDS AND
FELLOW SURVIVOR

SO-BYW-969

SURVIVOR
LOVE
THY ENEMY

JAMES DENNISON

Copyright © 2012 James Dennison
All rights reserved.

ISBN: 1477478159
ISBN 13: 9781477478158

DEDICATION

*To my son, Christopher whose passing
motivated me to face the demons of my past*

*"The rythm of our writing flows from
the souls of those who have passed."*

CHAPTER

1

I am a sacrificial lamb to the gods of war. On May 17, 1966, I was drafted in Chicago at the age of twenty with many other young men and transported to Fort Riley, Kansas, where the Ninth Infantry Division was forming and preparing to go to Vietnam. We were all convinced that we would not be placed into the infantry, even if we did go to Vietnam.

On the first day of basic training, the first sergeant, who stood six foot seven and weighed about 275 pounds, addressed the company. "My name is Lynn D. Crockett, and the first one to call me Davey gets this black boot up his ass!" That was when I first yearned for my mother.

The next thing I knew, my bayonet was up against my throat, and a voice said, "You are a dead son of a bitch." I had left my scabbard unbuckled, and Terry McBride, a legitimate Hell's Angel, had slipped my bayonet out of my scabbard and placed it against my throat: a fine introduction to the infantry.

Training consisted of three-mile runs, physical training, and mental harassment. We spit-shined the barracks until 10:00 p.m.

Then we got up at 5:00 a.m. to do it all over again. By the end of the first week, most of us had ceased to upchuck our breakfast and were ready to intensify our training. The second week of basic, we started close-order drill, more running, physical training, and three-mile marches. This was broken up by boring classes on hand grenades, booby traps, claymore mines, and other assorted obstacles we might encounter. It became increasingly apparent that we were bound for Vietnam.

The third week of basic training included more of the same plus our first venture bivouac (camping out). This was also our first introduction to C rations (meals in a can): ham, lima beans, and fat; hot dogs and fat; meat balls and fat—you get the idea. Our first reaction to the food was dysentery. I'd fly out of my tent at 6:00 a.m., drop my drawers, and go into a three-point squat with everything running out of me.

One time a lieutenant walked by, sunglasses and all, and saluted me. One always has to salute an officer, and there I was in a three-point squat. The officer held the salute for a long time, just waiting for me to fall into my own excrement, relishing the sounds of my evacuation. He never cracked a smile. Finally, he broke the salute and marched off with a good story to tell his buddies. I resolved to only evacuate myself in the middle of the night from then on.

Since my platoon (First) was always screwing up, we regularly received extra exercise while everyone else relaxed. Our best drill instructor, Sgt. Johnson, was in perfect physical condition. All business, he never smiled—except when conducting extra drills for the First Platoon. Then he would smile, his gold tooth would glisten in the sun, and he would say, "Your ass is mine" and run us ragged.

I happened to run into a guy from my block in the records department one day. He checked my MOS (Military Occupation Code) and told me I was going to be the company clerk. This was good news. While the rest of the platoon sweated it out in the infantry, I had confidence I would be rear echelon.

The following week, we went to rifle qualification. Bored to death, we put together a kitty: Whoever shot best got ten dollars, and second place got five. I shot my ass off and got five bucks. The platoon sergeant called me out in front of the unit the next morning. He congratulated me on my marksmanship and informed me that I *was* going to be Company clerk, but, because of my marksmanship, I would now be a machine gunner instead. All for a lousy five bucks.

The rest of basic was pretty routine except for one exercise: the obstacle course. It consisted of about a mile of malicious obstacles we had to navigate while wearing eighty-pound backpacks and carrying fixed bayonets in the ninety-degree heat. I thought I was going to die. Then our sympathetic captain had us do it again. Mother of God!

After semirecuperating, I wandered off to the only tree in sight and cried like a baby. "I can't kill anybody," I said to myself. I cried for a good minutes before I returned to my brothers. I had finally succumbed to the god of war.

In April 1967, Company C had been on and off Vietnam's Thoi Son Island for more than a month. The island just south of the Rung Sat—Swamp of the Assassins—was a salt water swamp about twenty miles south of Saigon. Closer still was the US Ninth Infantry Division's base camp at Dong Tam. square miles of rubber plantation and orchards, the small, insignificant island made the perfect staging area for Viet Cong guerrilla mortar attacks on Americans. Adding to the confusion, the Cong sent nightly guerrilla attacks through the swamps using hit-and-run tactics.

So far, Charlie Company had lost ten men to a combination of booby traps and sniper fire. Yet despite Thoi Son Island's status as a known enemy sanctuary, the soldiers of Charlie Company could never find any evidence of the scale of the Cong units—only mud, leeches, red ants, heat exhaustion, dehydration, snipers, and, of course, booby traps.

"Who's got first watch?" I asked.

"I do," Mike O'Leary grunted in reply. "I'll take the first two hours."

He figured he would rather have first watch and then get some sleep than face the all-encompassing jungle darkness. "Y'all go ahead with your wet dreams while I protect you."

The day had started at 6:00 a.m. with cold C rations followed by hours of slogging through the mud in one-hundred-degree heat and 100 percent humidity. We encountered bloodsuckers, mud, and combat—all on no more than six hours' sleep. As O'Leary ate cold US Army C rations, he set up some claymore mines. Claymores were electronically detonated dynamite units packed with buckshot—nasty killing and maiming devices.

Hidden away several meters below ground in a nearby tunnel, Viet Cong loyalist Van Nguyen prepared to ambush the Americans Like his counterparts only a few yards away, Van worked on his implements for killing: homemade booby traps and claymore mines created from C ration cans, ball bearings, and C-4 explosives and blasting caps provided by the barber at the American base camp at Dong Tam. The Cong could often count on the civilian population for help and support, mostly through intimidation, but not always. Many Vietnamese were pragmatists—someone was going to win this war, so, when necessary, it made sense to work both sides.

Van burned with primordial fire for the Viet Cong and its revolution. He longed for the expected eventual takeover by the North Vietnamese Communists. The Viet Cong, a guerrilla force dedicated to the ousting of Western influence in Vietnam, was supplied and funded by North Vietnam. The French were driven out in 1954 from what was then known as "French Indo-China." In 1967, it was the Americans who had to be eliminated. Van and his compatriots dreamed of reuniting the North and the South into one country: Vietnam.

Van's earliest memories included war. His father, Tuyen Plan, owned a rubber plantation on Thoi Son Island but died when Van was very young. Van's older brother, Cam Nguyen, served near Saigon with the South Vietnam forces, Army of the Republic of Vietnam (ARVN), and his mother, Qui, continued living on Thoi Son Island.

Van had been indoctrinated by the Communists. He believed the capitalist forces were at work in his country and should be driven out. He, like most of his fellow countrymen, had a historical distrust of the Chinese and felt confident Vietnam could be self-sufficient, both economically and politically, once the revolution was successful.

Now, Van armed himself with an American-made M-1 carbine, which he kept meticulously clean. He depended on it to assassinate Americans. He had been trained by one of the best snipers in Vietnam, had a sufficient supply of ammo, and, having grown up on the island, knew it like the back of his hand.

Van was in charge of a cadre of ten Viet Cong who had been harassing and killing Americans since they first began patrolling the island two months earlier. He slept intermittently in his dark tunnel, where it was always night, and dreamed of killing another American, which was easy—their sloppy habits told him exactly where they were. He had to admit, though, that the Yankees made very good weapons. His carbine had been more than reliable. One round was all it took, and he could chalk up another kill using the enemy's own rifle.

Van's mother, Qui, had lived a lonely life on Thoi Son Island. Thin in stature with long, dark hair and almond eyes, the family's matriarch was a great beauty. At age seventeen, she was betrothed in a Buddhist ceremony through an arranged marriage to the wealthy Tuyen Plan, twenty years her senior. Plan was a kind, spiritual man, and the newlywed couple quickly became the proud parents of two sons: Cam and Van.

Plan loved his plantation, which covered more than half the island. His death was attributed to malaria, but the Viet Cong takeover of the island had much to do with his demise. Qui felt her husband's despair included the psychological death of their son, Van, who had bought into the Communist propaganda machine. Cam, their eldest son, excelled in Officer Candidate School (OCS) and became an infantry first lieutenant stationed near Saigon.

Qui was very proud of Cam, but Van was another story. He had always been rebellious, but especially since he was fifteen, when the Communist revolution engulfed life on Thoi Son Island. Van swallowed all of the propaganda sent down from the North. He was taught the only hope for the masses was community ownership of land and materials; that the western powers only wished to rape Vietnam of its natural resources and women; that only the Communist hierarchy knew what was best for the masses; and that all forms of religion were merely a means of mind control.

Life on Thai Son Island revolved around the furtherance of the Communist way of life through ousting the Americans. Having seen the corruption of the Saigon government and the plight of the peasants, Van devoted himself to learning Communist theory and adopted the conviction that Vietnam would be self-governing.

His mother, Qui, accepted some of the Communists' theories but could not accept the violence and atrocities they committed against the Vietnamese people. Qui had not seen or heard from Van in five years, although he was often just a few miles away. She didn't know where Van was or what he was doing, but she loved him deeply, prayed for peace, and sympathized with both the South Vietnamese cause and the Viet Cong. As a mother, she recognized the pain of all mothers whose sons were in jeopardy.

The night passed uneventfully as the usual sounds of the jungle dominated my world. I was elated to hear that the boats would pick up me and my comrades shortly after noon to take us back to the *USS Benowah*. We would have a few days off to clean up, get three hot meals, and sleep on clean sheets, and we would have plenty of time to write home.

The Riverine force had been formed in early 1967, and the *Benowah* was the barracks ship upon which lived some five hundred US Army ground-pounders of the Second Brigade, Ninth Infantry Division. We were deployed for three to four days at a time in the Rung Sat, a saltwater swamp where the Viet Cong stored large caches of supplies and ammunition.

Having lost many comrades on the previous mission, including my three best friends, I became extremely depressed. "When will my number be up?" I wondered. It was midday, and I had been out of water for several hours. The sweat poured off my body. The platoon took a break in the local village square, and all I wanted was to get to the boat and have a drink of fresh water.

Meanwhile, close behind, Van had been trailing the American column since daylight. He noticed the American soldiers had quickened their pace using the main trails. They were obviously heading to a pickup point, preparing to leave the island. Van had missed several opportunities to kill another American soldier, but the conditions had not been right. As he watched the Americans

6

take a break in his home village, he was determined to strike, no matter the cost.

Qui watched as the line of American soldiers wound through town. Her heart went out to them as, drenched in sweat, they labored under heavy packs. Qui saw her own sons in all of the Americans. One soldier in particular, the one who looked especially thirsty and tired, reminded Qui of her Van, Qui drew cool water from the well and approached him, her eyes filled with love and compassion.

At the edge of the jungle, Van placed himself into a sniper's position and took careful aim. A single shot rang out, but it hadn't come from the Viet Cong guerrilla. Van screamed out in severe pain. He had been outsmarted—shot in the right shoulder by an American soldier who had spotted him in the jungle.

Van escaped by slipping into a tunnel leading to the adjoining town. He sought the aid of Tuyen, with whom he'd had an ongoing love affair since they were fifteen. Tuyen got a sympathetic Vietnamese doctor to remove the American bullet from Van's shoulder. Unfortunately for the Americans, he would recover completely.

Van stayed with Tuyen for a month, gathering his strength and filling his days by imparting more Communist indoctrination to her. During that time, Van and Tuyen committed themselves to each other. Van concentrated his full attention on the revolution at hand. When he was able, they discussed the Communist philosophy and the progress of the war.

"Why do you think Vietnam is crucial in the advance of the Communist cause in Asia?" Van asked.

"It is quite important that the world sees that communism can motivate the common people of Vietnam to overthrow Capitalist rule and become an independent country," Tuyen responded.

When he had fully recovered, Van reported to his superior, Colonel Khan in Saigon, for further assignment in the Mekong Delta, where Colonel Khan promoted him to lieutenant.

CHAPTER
2

Growing up on Chicago's north side with a father who owned a bar was a dream for most young men, and I took full advantage of the situation by drinking up most of my Dad's profits. My mother worked as a bookkeeper out of necessity. A sister seven years my senior rounded out our family. She was loving but somewhat distant.

I attended Catholic schools, where I became a victim of Catholic guilt and the fear of eternal damnation. Mine was a typical Catholic school boy's life. In grammar school, I was an altar boy and played in the school band. Although I was quite bright compared to the other students, I did just enough to get by—in both my studies and life in general. Unlike my athletic father, I was uncoordinated. I preferred to read, soaking up anything with words I could get my hands on. Despite my good looks, I was extremely shy during my formative years and tended to be a loner.

Aside from devouring a good book, my greatest joy was fishing at a small lake in nearby Wisconsin, where my parents owned a summer cottage. While I was barely noticed in my neighborhood during my school days in Chicago and had few friends, in Wisconsin, I was quite popular, becoming the center of attention amid the many friends I made during vacation trips north. This social schism created a split personality.

After high school, I attended the University of Illinois's Chicago campus, where I majored in engineering. I quickly assessed that I had no aptitude for this rather intense subject, whereupon I immediately switched to liberal arts. There was, however, a problem with that decision: the college of liberal arts required a foreign language in order to graduate. I enrolled late in a French class, which put me two weeks behind. Although I did quite well in my other subjects, poor grades in French got me placed on probation. Eventually, I flunked out.

My three best friends were drafted in 1966, landing in the Marine Corps. My response to their situation was, "Your ass is grass. You will be in Vietnam in the infantry in twelve weeks." I was sure that I, however, would not be placed in the infantry.

The draft was first instituted in World War I. It was resurrected in 1940, just prior to World War II, and continued on into the 1970s. Everyone eligible for the draft could stay out of the military if they attended school full-time. If one joined the Air Force, Navy, or Marines, their enlistment was four years. If drafted, enlistment was two years—and you were much more likely to be placed in the infantry. I laughed my ass off because I knew I was too smart to be placed in the infantry.

I returned to the auto parts store I had worked at part-time since I was sixteen. There I met Jeri, the eighteen-year-old Italian-America daughter of one of the employees. She was quite beautiful and intelligent, and we immediately fell in love. Shortly thereafter, in May of 1966, I was drafted and sent to Fort Riley, Kansas. The Ninth Infantry Division was forming for Vietnam, and, to my surprise, I was to be a part of it.

After the first stage of Basic Training, the new soldiers were granted two weeks of leave. This time was filled with both joy and depression—happiness at being home among family and friends and sorrow at the realization of what lay ahead in the jungles of Vietnam. I spent the majority of that time with Jeri. During my last weekend before returning to duty, Jeri and I retreated to the family cottage in Wisconsin. After a wonderful day of eating, drinking, and serious foreplay, we sat on the shore of the lake. I informed her it would not be wise to wait for me because, even if I did return, I probably would not be the same man who'd left her. Jeri told me she would always love me no matter what, and the subject was dropped.

The final week of furlough passed swiftly, and soon, I found myself back in the throes of a hectic training schedule. We spent the next sixteen weeks in advanced infantry training. Ironically, those final weeks of training were of great benefit to Charlie Company. We were bonding and becoming a true band of brothers. The 9th Division trained as a unit for thirty-two weeks, and, by the end of that time, it had become a fully-integrated fighting unit, each company having expunged its misfits.

Charlie Company was informed it would become part of the Mobile Riverine Force (MRF), based in the Mekong Delta. The unit was to operate from US Navy gunboats. The MRF unit was an amalgam of concepts dating back to the Civil War and influenced by the operation of French Riverine units in the '40s and '50s during World War II and France's war with the Viet Cong in a futile attempt to save their French Indo-China colony (now Vietnam) from the Communists.

By now, each member of Charlie Company had resigned himself to going to war in Vietnam, but what would that be like? The big concern was that, thus far, we hadn't had any jungle training. There just weren't a lot of jungles to train in on the plains of Kansas. The unit sent a signed letter to the brigade's commanding officer, Colonel Fulton, requesting jungle training. The following morning, the Colonel replied by addressing Company C. He agreed with their concerns and promised that "things will change." The result was that Company C ran five miles each morning instead of three.

At the end of November, we went to Brigade Combat Qualifications, which would certify the unit "combat ready." During the combat qualifications, my squad was assigned to ambush an armored personnel unit that was to come through a gorge at 0700 hours (7:00 a.m.). True to Army form, the target didn't arrive until 0900 hours. When the ambush was sprung, everyone in the squad was cramped up from the cold. After the ambush, my squad departed knowing that, if captured, we would be subject to a beating, even though it was only a war game. Loaded down with an M-14 rifle, eight hundred rounds of machine gun ammo, and a backpack, I carried a total weight of about sixty pounds. My machine gunner had only an M-60 machine gun to carry, but not without a lot of pissing and moaning.

As I made my escape from the ambush, I abandoned my weapon and all my gear at the ambush site and headed to Chicago for a scheduled break. My abandoned gear was found. That news had to be reported to the squad leaders, who, in turn, informed the Company lieutenant. Word made its way up the chain of command all the way to the brigade commander. The exercise was called off, and my gear was retrieved—as was I. I spent a lot of time doing extra duty over the next few weeks.

At the end of training, Charlie Company received a sumptuous Thanksgiving dinner where the company commander addressed the men, informing them that anyone who needed extra leave time should inform his squad leader, and they would be accommodated.

I immediately ran across the street to a pay phone and called my mother. I told her that if anyone called from Company C asking if my sister was getting married the next weekend, please confirm it.

I got to go home a week before everyone else, but I was charged for the extra leave at the other end of my time in the Army before being discharged. Those forty days of leave were bittersweet. I spent most of my time with Jeri while I made the obligatory round of good-byes to relatives and those friends not already serving in the military.

I discovered that my three best friends, who had been drafted into the Marine Corps, had landed sweetheart assignments. One was stationed at Twenty-Nine Palms, California, where he was in charge of the beer hall; another went to Norfolk, where he off-loaded planes from aircraft carriers; and the third went to Okinawa. Somehow, there was an unwritten rule that no Marine Corps draftees went to Vietnam—although that policy would later change.

Other friends had been assigned as cooks and company clerks. As luck would have it, I was the only one headed for combat.

Jeri was more in love with me than ever and wanted to spend all her time with me, which hurt her studies at the University of Illinois. Already on probation, she received a notice of expulsion before I left. Jeri's love had become intense, which made me feel imprisoned. Although I had very deep feelings for her, the stark reality of being shipped far away to be shot at made it hard for me to distinguish between love and loneliness.

We spent many hours talking about the future. I discouraged any idea of total commitment, while Jeri hoped for a wedding ring. I was unprepared to make that vow. Those days of leave passed quickly, and suddenly, it was time to return to Fort Riley. On our last night together, I took Jeri to see *The Sand Pebbles*. During intermission, we left the theatre promising each other we'd see the second half of the movie together upon my return from Vietnam. Upon saying good-bye to Jeri and turning to walk away, a cold rush went over me. I wondered, "Will I ever return?"

CHAPTER

3

On January 9, 1967, the Second Brigade took the train from Ft. Riley to the port of Oakland, California, to board the *USS John S. Pope*, a World War II "liberty" troop ship. Some three thousand Army troops walked aboard, each carrying full equipment, all headed for Vietnam. We all figured we would be let off the train in Oakland for some liberty to do some last-minute partying before debarkation into unknown waters, but that was not to be. The troop train backed up directly to the ship, and we boarded immediately. We landlocked soldiers from the middle of the country were expecting sea-sickness as the ship left the dock. When that didn't occur, we decided the stories of seasickness dispensed by crusty old sergeants were simply more scuttlebutt propaganda. The next morning, however, many of the soldiers were sea-sick. Though we didn't know it, the ship was still in San Francisco Bay. Once we hit the high seas, the real journey began.

Upon boarding the ship and stowing my gear, I took the advice of old Navy veterans and sought out the top bunk in the four-stacked berthing facilities. It didn't take long for me to realize why that was a good idea. The men in the lower bunks were inundated by vomit from those above. The fifty-two members of the platoon were crammed into a twenty-five hundred square-foot space. The closed-in surroundings and rolling of the ship ensured that no one was able to eat for two days.

At breakfast on the third day, I was finally ready to stomach some food. Of course, I had to stand in a chow line for two hours first. I took a box of corn flakes and an apple, but as I sat down and slid my cereal bowl into the slot in the table, a fellow soldier sitting next to me vomited into his bowl. Those first few days were rugged for us Fort Riley ground pounders.

Eventually, shipboard life settled into a daily routine during the long, arduous trip across the Pacific. After about five days, I could finally go to the bathroom. Those facilities were Spartan at best. The "toilets" were simply long boards with holes cut in them over troughs. I sat down to relieve myself just as a large wave hit the ship, sending all the vomit and excrement surging out of the trough. Oh, happy day!

Upon finally reaching Okinawa in the Japanese island chain on the far side of the Pacific, everyone eagerly got off the ship for a much-needed eight-hour liberty. The majority of the soldiers came back with bottles of Japanese sake—not exactly a remedy for the lingering sea sickness.

As the ship sailed ever closer to the Indo-China coastline, the reality of war began to sink in. As we slept the night after leaving Okinawa, all the lights came on and the air raid sirens sounded. It was no drill. After some excitement, we settled back down.

Other than fear of the unknown fast approaching us, the most important thing on our minds was food. We could never get enough food on the ship. One of the soldiers got drunk on the sake he had smuggled aboard and broke into the ship's galley. Marine guards grabbed him immediately, but he broke away and dove over the side into the dark ocean.

By maritime law, the Navy had to search for the man for up to three days. Realizing this could be a clever tactic for delaying the inevitable, several of the soldiers decided to draw straws and throw some poor bastard overboard every three days. They figured that by doing this, they would never get to Vietnam. Besides, they would have far fewer casualties at sea than they were expecting fighting in the jungles of Vietnam. Unfortunately, it was just a dream.

The huge troop ship finally arrived in Vung Tau some twenty-eight days after leaving Oakland Army Terminal. We debarked the ship and were taken to our base at Camp Bearcat. We spent the next several weeks building barracks and becoming accustomed to the hot, humid climate of South Vietnam. After filling hundreds of sandbags and doing limited patrol duty outside of Bearcat, Charlie Company was sent on its first patrol with an armored personnel carrier. After twelve hours, we proceeded to dig foxholes for the night. The thought of sleeping in a hole with the enemy and all sorts of strange bugs and creatures lurking about had everyone in the patrol scared shitless. The jungle was scary enough in the daylight, but at night, the sounds intensified and the surrounding darkness became engulfing.

About an hour after dark, we heard voices coming from the jungle. From around the perimeter, the men of Charlie Company heard the familiar Yankee expression "fuck: "Fuck you; fuck you." The Viet Cong had learned just enough English to piss off a dog-face. Immediately, everyone commenced firing. After five minutes, a cease-fire was called. We received no incoming rounds.

The perceived cat calls started up again. We barely slept. When daylight arrived, we learned our first lesson in the strange ways of the jungle. A group of small lizards had been mating the night before, and, appropriately enough, the sound they make sounds just like they are saying, "Fuck you." One Texan grunted matter-of- factly, "They musta' been horny frogs from TCU." After that night, the reptiles would forever be known to the men of Charlie Company as the "fuck you" lizards.

Patrol began again. The TET holiday, the lunar New Year celebration for the Vietnamese, usually meant a cease-fire by all combatants. The first platoon was sent out on patrol with orders to go about two hundred meters and set up an ambush. After traveling that distance, the soldiers found themselves knee deep in water—waist deep in some places. Every fifty meters, they had to cross a drainage canal. By midnight, the platoon was lost, stretched out

17

over the two hundred meters. The men in the rear were yelling, "Wait for me assholes!" So much for noise control.

Finally, at 3 a.m., the platoon found a dry knoll, and everyone but the duty guards passed out. At daylight, they carefully looked around where they had been sleeping and saw their own main encampment one hundred meters away. Had they continued moving the night before, they would have been decimated by their own men. After the TET holiday, Charlie Company boarded the *USS Benewah*—their barracks ship, their home away from home—and began operations on Thoi Son Island.

CHAPTER

4

Mike grew up in a small, conservative farming community in Iowa with about five thousand people, ten churches, and twenty bars. Everyone knew everyone else and liked it that way. The folks loved local and state football, knew all the players' names, and frowned on any ideas coming out of the big city. An average kid, Mike was popular with the girls and did not like school.

After graduation, he worked farm jobs, got semiserious with some of the farm girls, and waited for the draft. Everyone else loved the quiet life of his hometown, but he was bored to death. He wanted to get involved with law enforcement after he served his time in the military, with the ultimate goal of becoming county sheriff. Mike welcomed the Army when it came calling and looked forward to serving in Vietnam and fighting for his country.

Juan came from a typical southwestern Texas family. His father worked the fields while his mother took care of the house and her seven children. Juan's was a conservative Catholic family, abiding by the laws and respecting the government. He performed as lead guitarist in a rock and roll band. The group was popular locally, and they dreamed of hitting the big time after their military service. Juan thought about joining the Air Force or Navy but didn't want to commit to the extra two years and didn't think that he would be put in the infantry.

He only went out with Mexican girls who were committed to virginity, so his was a sexually powerful yet frustrating life. Juan was resigned to being drafted, and when he found out that he was headed for Vietnam in the infantry, he was sure he'd be protected by the God he loved and his mother's prayers.

Willy was a gang banger from Chicago. Willy never knew his father and was one of ten children his mother had by four different fathers. He was born in the middle of the tribe, and his had always been a street existence. Willy dropped out of school after the tenth grade, not because he was stupid but because he was bored and saw that there was money to be made selling drugs and strong arming businesses. His last go-round with the police resulted in his volunteering for the Army. Unlike most of us, Willy was pleased to learn that he was being sent to Vietnam in the infantry. This experience would improve his reputation on the street and make him a big shot back on the block.

Then there was John, a surfer dude and ladies' man from Southern California. School only interfered with his surfing, and any communication from the draft board was easily ignored. The Army got John's attention when the Military Police showed up on the beach one day. His first inclination was to escape to Canada on his surf board, but it soon became obvious that was not feasible. John succumbed to the power of the government and quickly found himself in Vietnam.

Mike was damned tired of the M-60 machine gun. Not only did it weigh thirty-five pounds unloaded, it was an obvious target for the enemy and a bitch to keep clean and functioning. Now it seemed that war was the only life he had ever known and home was a figment of his imagination. Mike's only solace was the letters that kept coming from home, assuring him that the United States was indeed real and that someday he would return.

"Did you hear that crocodile swishing back and forth in the water last night?" Mike asked no one in particular.

"That wasn't a crocodile; it was two monkeys screwing each other," someone replied.

"That wasn't a crocodile, it was Mike screwing a monkey; he's pretty hard up," another voice added.

Mike threw his canteen at his accuser and said, "Screw you guys! You know I've got a reputation to maintain back home with the ladies."

Ah, those home-grown ladies. Mike had done his best to sow his seed with every girl in the area, taking advantage of the sympathy that came with heading into combat.

"I hope I never see another Viet Cong or hear another rifle the rest of my life," he said. "I'll be happy to slog through mud, eat C rations, carry one-hundred-pound packs, and survive on four hours' sleep a night for the rest of my tour as long as I make it home OK."

No one responded. This was wishful thinking and something we'd all thought about. Mike retreated further into his own daydreams about girls and home, gradually removing himself from the horrors of day-to-day existence. This was extremely dangerous. The less time a soldier pays to his current situation, the more likely he is to make mistakes—the more likely he is to die.

Since Mike took the first watch, he was the last to be awakened as the harsh Mekong Delta sun rose to greet the men of Charlie Company. The tide had receded, leaving gut-sucking mud to wade through as another hellish day began. The only good was that each day was a day closer to home, dead, wounded, or crazy. The first order of business was to strip naked and inspect each other for the bloodsuckers that had been consuming us all night. We took turns in pairs burning off the amoebas that had gotten fat on us. This was our most vulnerable time, since half the platoon was without weapons while checking out their buddies, and the other half was busy accomplishing this act of purification. No one paid much attention to danger.

Van, aware of their routine, perched patiently in a tree twenty-five meters away. "Get the bloodsuckers off my neck," were the last words Mike ever spoke. One shot broke the stillness of the jungle, and he crumbled to the ground. "Medic! Medic! Mike's been shot in the chest!"

Doc ran up and checked for a pulse, but nothing could help Mike. His aorta had exploded. Our platoon opened up with everything we had in the direction the shot had come from, but Van had disappeared into another tunnel hide-away, secure in the knowledge that he had another kill.

The stupid Americans never changed their habits. They checked for bloodsuckers, ate breakfast, smoked a cigarette, and loaded up for the day. It made sniping like shooting ducks in a pond. Mike's small town had lost its future chief of police.

CHAPTER

5

The Company returned to the *USS Benowah* for several days of drying out. After cleaning weapons, gear, and bodies, we ate our first real meal in some time. Sleep had become paramount to everyone, and the sleeping area resounded with snores and deep breathing, punctuated by the moans of those reliving their mission.

The cloud of another mission loomed on the horizon for everyone. This was the time I was most afraid, lying in my bunk in the dark, letting my imagination run wild, thinking through every possible "what if."

The next few days were filled with checking gear; writing letters home and, hopefully, receiving some; being briefed on the next mission; and dreading it. On the fourth day, the Company debarked for another week of patrol on Thoi Son Island. As usual, we were all very professional upon beginning the patrol, being well rested and on full alert.

One of the deceiving things about living on the ship was how it messed with your mind. After dealing with life in a hellish jungle for several days, we psychologically returned to the land of the big PX. The drawback to this was that instead of adjusting to the reality of combat in eighty- to ninety-day continuous patrols as a normal infantry unit did, the troops of the Riverine force were constantly influenced by the false luxury of our two- to three-day returns to the lap of luxury.

Juan proceeded to clean his M-16. He was small and immature for his age and was therefore the subject of much abuse from his fellow platoon members. "Hey, Mex, you screw any sheep when you were living on the Rio Grande, or was it just Indian squaws?"

Juan was embarrassed by these questions, having adhered to his family's strict Catholic tradition. He was saving himself for his future wife and did not drink, smoke, do drugs, or fool around with the local whores. He was proud of his virginity and his Mexican heritage, and although he had no senorita waiting for him back home, he planned on finding one as soon he returned and immersing himself in family life.

He had killed when he'd needed to but tried to support the poor local Vietnamese villagers whenever possible. He identified with them and saw in them the same desires and soul that poor Mexicans crossing the border had. He had no hate for them, only sympathy and a common humanity. He realized that a great many were Viet Cong sympathizers but viewed that as a personal choice.

Members of the platoon were constantly ragging on each other with racial epithets, but in the context of combat, Juan knew that was only a means of relieving tension. He loved his comrades as himself and would've done anything for them.

He constantly thought of the eight months remaining on his tour of duty. He had already picked out the members of his future band: Carlos on lead guitar, Jose on sax, Jaime on keyboard, and he would play drums. He knew they were going to make a fortune. He tried not to think about the future too much because the first order of business was surviving that hellhole. Too many experienced troops had died recently, and paying attention to survival was foremost in his mind. He had a difficult time identifying with replacement troops because he knew many of them would die.

Juan's loyalty was to the original platoon he'd trained with, and out of the original fifty-five, thirty remained.

Van had been watching the American troopers for some time and was now disappointed by their attention to survival. He searched for a new plan of attack. He'd noticed through the course of time that the Company was most vulnerable at midday, when they'd break for lunch after slogging through mud and one-hundred-degree heat for six hours. The Company was entering an area of Thoi Son Island that consisted of much thicker jungle, impossible to cut through, forcing them to stick to existing trails and take breaks in clearings.

Word came down to break for lunch. It was high noon, and the heat and humidity were relentless. Juan checked his C rations and was disappointed to find that he had a magnificent meal of ham and lima beans, his least favorite. He gagged it down and finished it off with hot water from his canteen. Hunger and dehydration made a man accept anything.

After eating, he stood up and stretched near three of his closest friends. Just then, Van threw a live grenade into their midst. Against all training procedures, Juan threw himself onto the grenade, saving his friends. The band had lost its drummer forever.

John found military life terribly restrictive. Accustomed to the carefree lifestyle of a Southern California surfer, he rebelled at the discipline and conformity required. As a result, he was unable to rise in the ranks as his fellow troopers did. This did not disturb him, as the last thing he wanted was to be in charge of or responsible for one of his companions' deaths. John was gifted physically and possessed an above-average IQ and strong leadership qualities. The noncommissioned officers expected John to assume a role of responsibility, which resulted in constant conflict with his superiors. All through training, John was the odd man out, looked up to by his fellow soldiers but always derided by his superiors.

Once in Vietnam, John blended into the background, volunteering for point so that he could constantly be aware of what was going on. Patrolling Thoi Son Island, he spotted a Viet Cong across the river with a weapon. We piled our gear on the rafts we carried with us and regrouped across the river. A box of machine-gun ammo slipped into the river, and our platoon had to delay in order to retrieve it. Once regrouped, we moved up the muddy bank.

Suddenly, a shot rang out. That happened all the time, with troops having their weapons off safety and inadvertently firing off a round. We each turned to the fellow next to us and wanted to know who the dumb shit was that time. A whistle went off on the other side of the river—and the world exploded. The platoon had been drawn into an ambush by the VC. Machine guns, mortars, and rockets exploded everywhere.

We returned fire and called in artillery on ourselves. After what seemed like an eternity, but in reality was only five minutes, we heard the whistle again over all the noise and the attack stopped. Our platoon suffered two wounded, who needed to be evacuated. John felt a warmth between his legs and thought he had been wounded. Turns out, he had shit his pants. We set up camp for the night, realizing the enemy knew exactly where we were.

As we crossed the river again the next day, word came down to head for a pickup point by the boats. We came across a bombed-out clearing, which we would normally go around because of the potential for booby traps, but since we had to meet the boats, we went straight through it. As John crossed into the wood line, the man behind him tripped a booby trap, wounding three other troopers. As those wounded were being medivacked out, the rest of the platoon sat down in place as we had been trained to do. John never saw the booby trap he sat on. He only heard the explosion and became another member on the long list of KIA (Killed In Action) from Charlie Company. Someone else would have to ride his waves.

Willy was a lean, mean machine. Although he hated the conditions we had to live in—red ants swarming on you by the thousands, bloodsuckers at night, mosquitoes all the time, heat, humidity, and always mud—he enjoyed the rhythm of military life and the organizational skills it taught him. He knew this would be beneficial when he returned to the block a war hero, with the rest of the hood controlled by himself and his underlings. Whatever opposition he encountered upon his return home, he would eliminate, just as he had eliminated the enemy in Vietnam and accomplished what he wanted. He studied how the Viet Cong operated and respected their resilience and patience. Jungle warfare tactics were how he planned to take over the hood.

Willy received many letters from girlfriends and gang bangers but really only looked forward to the letters from his mom. She had been an addict all her life, but he loved her deeply and protected her when he was home. When he took over the hood, he was going to buy her a big house on the right side of town and get her into rehab. She was only thirty-five but looked sixty. Willy didn't use drugs himself, having seen the ravages they wrought in the hood. Drugs were a means to an end.

We came to the river's edge around 2:00 p.m. It had been ten days since John's death, and we had each cried our tears and secretly thanked God it was him and not us.

The Company returned to its normal routine, and Van took note of their sloppiness from his hidden location. The captain decided to let the men cease operations early to do maintenance on their weapons and bodies and catch up on some sleep.

About three hundred meters further on was the village where Van had recuperated from his wounds. Women, children, and old men populated it. All the young men had joined the Viet Cong. Tuyen had lived in the village all her life, and her entire family and village were Viet Cong. Now, at seventeen, she stood five feet six inches tall, had long black hair, and weighed about 110 pounds. For as long as she could remember, there had been war—first by the French and then by the Americans. Tuyen hated the Americans with her entire being and was determined to do anything to further the Communist cause. She had been indoctrinated by Van in the principles of Communism and lived in the fire of her conviction.

She smiled as she saw the Americans set up early by the river and realized that they would be there for some time. She was willing to make the ultimate sacrifice if necessary. Van had been trailing the Americans after John's death. As usual, the Americans had become very professional after John's death, but they soon became sloppy again. Van had been plotting with Tuyen to ambush an American soldier and was waiting for the perfect time. He made contact with Tuyen and set up his claymore mine.

Willy was pleased to set up early for a change. The patrol had been one long march through the jungles and swamps of Thoi Son Island with nothing to show for it but five KIA and ten wounded. Willy was hoping to get back to the *USS Benowah* soon to smoke some grass and listen to some good Jazz. Just after he had consumed his C rations and cleaned up, he noticed Tuyen emerge from the village. She said, "GI number one, bang bang, two dollar."

Willy realized he was in a position to have some sexual gratification even in this remote area. Never one to turn down such an opportunity, he called out to the men on either side of his position that he was going out to get some poontang and not to mistake him for a Viet Cong when he returned.

As Willy approached Tuyen, Van detonated his claymore mine from a distance of four meters. Willy's fellow soldiers heard the explosion, saw the puff of smoke, and heard him scream, "I only wanted to have some fun in this God awful place!" Doc was the first to get to him. Willy's legs had been blown off from the knees down, and his right arm was severed at the elbow. Doc did what he could while waiting for the Medivac chopper, but Willy died of his wounds ten minutes later. The hood had lost its future president.

After participating in Willy's assassination, Tuyen reunited with Van in the tunnels undermining the village, where they vouchsafed their eternal love for each other but remained virginal due to Van's desire to save all of his physical and mental energies for the continuing effort to overthrow the allied forces controlling South Vietnam. Van departed after a week with Tuyen and followed his orders from the Communist High Command to report to Colonel Khan in Saigon for further training in the overthrow of the Saigon regime. Van was commissioned a lieutenant and given more responsibility.

CHAPTER

6

Tuyen was lost without Van and yearned for his return. After another month of loneliness, she was approached by the senior Viet Cong operative in the area. He told her that the Communist cadre was impressed by her beauty, intelligence, and commitment to the cause. They desired that she make a total commitment to Communism, leave her village where she had lived all her life, and proceed to Saigon for more in depth training. She agreed immediately. Her mother and siblings lived in the village, but her only wish was to help the Communist cause. She never looked back. She immediately went through an intense physical training program designed to prepare her for any contingency. She focused on self-defense training, sniper training, and, most importantly, mental toughening that would prepare her to have no emotional attachments. These activities took the better part of three months, and when the Communist cadre was through with her, she no longer recognized herself.

She spent her final month of indoctrination in Saigon learning the ways of a provocative spy. Tuyen improved her English, trained in manners, was indoctrinated into what a dedicated supporter of the South Vietnamese Government should believe, and, all in all, became everything she hated. A Communist spy had been created. During this period of time, Tuyen attracted the attention of many men, American and Vietnamese. She realized she could have anything she wanted from any man by using her feminine wiles and beauty. Sex was not a problem, as she really didn't enjoy it and was totally committed to Van. Tuyen didn't realize she was playing a dangerous game that could get her killed. She had received no word of Van.

Soon she attracted the attention of Colonel Khan, who was in charge of all operations in the Mekong Delta. He fell madly in love with Tuyen, and it became a very secret liaison of great intensity. She easily fulfilled the yearnings of a man twenty years her senior whose entire life was devoted to the cause and desired a confidant for his dreams.

Tuyen eventually persuaded Colonel Khan to assign her to My Tho, an important town in the Mekong Delta where an American intelligence force was stationed and the opportunity for information gathering was great. Tuyen was placed with two other girls who knew nothing of her mission and was employed as a checkout girl at the main dispensary, where she would have a great deal of contact with American personnel. She also volunteered at the local hospital, where she would have close contact with the wounded. Tuyen looked forward to her first assignment, anticipating that someday, she would contribute greatly to the revolution.

Van, meanwhile, had been transferred to an area in Cambodia to train new recruits in the art of guerilla warfare. The Viet Cong had tunneled into the mountain for years, building medical facilities, training rooms, barracks, and rest and recuperation centers out of Mother Earth. No one knew the blueprints for these tunnels because the Vietnamese had built them over many years, burrowing in and tunneling until a cave-in and then tunneling in another direction. They were able to train in safety, since Cambodia was off limits to American ground troops. They were very security conscience since SOG (Special Operations Group) patrols searched constantly for Viet Cong sanctuaries to bomb.

Van thought about how stupid and naive the Americans were. They were allowed to fire only at Viet Cong who could be seen with a weapon, they could not bomb without permission from higher authority, and they couldn't interrogate prisoners without following the Geneva Conventions. It was like buying a teenager everything he wanted; supplying all the booze, women, and narcotics desired; and forbidding him to enjoy it. The Americans were suckers, even more so because they supplied the Saigon generals with all the money they could use with no oversight. And since the Saigon government was totally corrupt, the Communists knew it functioned only for its own gratification.

Lectures, field maneuvers, political indoctrination, and frustration filled Van's days. He enjoyed training the future revolutionaries and understood the need for his job, but his only real goal in life was to kill and destroy Americans. After four months of training the future revolutionaries, he was reassigned to the Mekong Delta and promoted to captain. There was a major action being planned against the Ninth Infantry Division Riverine force, which consisted of Army infantry stationed on navy boats. These were the same troops Van had decimated on Toy Son island, and he salivated at the thought of destroying them en masse.

Van's initial assignment was to observe and report on the Riverine force's activities. His analysis concluded that the Riverine troops were very disciplined, very well organized, and very committed. However, they suffered from the same problems that plagued all American troops: They were addicted to habit, doing the same things at the same time every day, and were limited in their operations by constantly having to function in mud and water.

The huge advantage the Americans had was the firepower they carried with them and the backup from the Monitor gunboats, which had dual quad fifty caliber machine guns and grenade launchers capable of firing a thousand rounds per minute. In addition, the Riverine force had the support of jets and artillery. The only way for the Viet Cong to be successful was to execute the perfect ambush.

The opportunity presented itself at the village of Ap Bac, a small village on the Ap Bac River that was preceded by a bend, shielding the town from sight. With flat, open spaces surrounded by mangrove trees, it was perfectly situated for an ambush. The Viet Cong had controlled the town for years. The local farmers cared not a whit who won the war, as they paid 40 percent of their crop to the Saigon government and 40 percent to the local Viet Cong, leaving them hardly enough to live on.

As this was virgin territory for the Riverine force, a great deal of time was spent analyzing the lay of the land and gaining insight into the attitudes of the local populace. Because of our extensive research about the area and its inhabitants, plans for the assault were in the hands of the local Viet Cong via spies in the South Vietnamese Army almost as soon as they were made.

The American High Command decided to make a major assault just east of the village of Ap Bac with three battalions of infantry in the early morning hours of June 19, 1967. The Riverine force left the *Benowah* at 0400 hours for the long journey to the area where the attack was to occur. We had never patrolled the Ap Bac area, and, to our knowledge, the only American forces ever there before were small groups of Navy SEALs. I realized that the platoon was being issued much larger amounts of ammunition than was the norm and knew that something big was in the offing.

The night before the mission, I shaved next to Anderson, one of the few remaining originals. Andy was one of the few members of the platoon able to grow a mustache, and he'd been grooming it into a beautiful handlebar. On that night, I noticed that Andy was shaving off his mustache. I immediately inquired as to why.

"I'm going to die tomorrow," Andy explained. "My wife hates my mustache, and I don't want her to see me in the coffin with it."

I was in disbelief. Andy was the acknowledged leader of the first platoon, husband to a beautiful woman, and father of a six-month-old baby boy—and he believed that he was not going to survive. I scoffed at the idea, and nothing more was said about it.

Charlie Company was to be inserted to the right of Alpha Company, separated only by a line of trees. To our front was another line of trees three hundred meters away. It was a broad open space, and it gave me the willies. I felt fortunate that the captain of Charlie Company had been with us since basic training and was a Mustang, which meant that he had been an enlisted man and then gone to Officers Candidate School. He knew all the tricks. The men of Charlie Company respected him implicitly and knew that if they were to survive, their chance of survival was greater with the commanders they had.

The Captain commanding A Company had attended the Air Force Academy in Colorado Springs and failed to make the grade. He then attended Officers Candidate School and was assigned to the infantry, rising in the ranks from second lieutenant to captain, just barely making the grade. The only reason he was in charge of an infantry company was that there was no one else left to do it.

This operation was his first combat experience. A Company had a history of being a bad-luck unit, pulling kitchen duty during the entire trip over on the troop ship. As soon as they exited the boats, the captain of Charlie Company sent out recon squads, which immediately saw signs of enemy activity. The squads slowed their pace to a crawl, making sure all the troops were dispersed and maintaining discipline. Fifteen minutes into the operation, tremendous gunfire erupted on their left flank, where Alpha Company was patrolling. It sounded to Tom as if his entire world was exploding. Charlie Company began to draw heavy gunfire from our immediate front and sides and slowly advanced up the tree lines, not out into the open rice paddies.

The firing over in the A Company sector continued unabated, with little return fire. It became apparent that they had walked into an ambush and were pinned down in the open rice paddies. Their rookie captain had led them out into the center of the rice paddies and when their point man had triggered the ambush when he came within ten meters of the far tree line.

Van was ecstatic. Through their contacts with the military planning arm of the South Vietnamese Army High Command, the Viet Cong had learned exactly where the Riverine force had planned to land at Ap Bac. Van had recruited three hundred Viet Cong encamped in bunkers surrounding one landing zone and three hundred more encircling the other. Each ambush team had four, fifty-caliber machine guns with plenty of ammo, and each troop was equipped with an automatic weapon.

Van manned the fifty-caliber machine gun at the center of the A Company ambush. He couldn't believe that the incompetent A Company captain had led his entire company into the center of the ambush with no recon. Van triggered the ambush, and within five minutes, all he could see were American bodies lying in the rice paddies. Surviving members of the A Company sent sporadic return fire, but nothing of consequence. Van signaled his men to continue firing into the remains of the American Company while there was limited resistance and no fire coming from the Monitor gunboats, which were still out on the river but approaching rapidly.

The surviving members of A Company tended to the wounded as well as could be expected while being constantly shot at from the wood line. Only 10 percent of the one hundred and fifty men that had constituted the company remained unharmed.

Meanwhile, some genius in High Command had decided sixteen-foot aluminum boats would be ideal for combat in the Mekong Delta. Joe, who served as a medic, thought the boats were good for duck hunting in New York, but God help you if there was a Viet Cong in the tree line of the Mekong Delta.

The weapons squad of ten men had entered a side tributary to the Bassac River just as the ambush was sprung. A Viet Cong in the tree line had a fifty caliber machine gun. All ten members of the weapons squad perished while Charlie Company endured withering fire from all sides. The Monitor gunships came to our aid, as there was no hope for the survivors of A Company. The Monitors pulled up to the shoreline as close to the action as possible. They unleashed a withering fire of fifty caliber machine guns while simultaneously pounding the enemy with one hundred rounds per minute of hand-grenade-size projectiles.

The assault helicopters arrived on the scene and began strafing the wood line incessantly. Two gunships were shot down, but more were coming. I was at the center of the action. I saw Andy go down immediately while trying to direct his squad during the assault and reflected on our conversation of the previous evening. I moved forward as ordered, taking no chances but doing as survival indicates. Charlie Company had not been able to move more than one hundred meters into the battlefield under the withering fire.

Our gunships were able to suppress some of the incoming fire, but the Medivac choppers were still unable to take out the wounded. Some of my buddies were bleeding to death. Then artillery commenced to pound the enemy, making a dent in their firepower.

Carlos had taken a bullet through the fleshy part of his right arm—a million-dollar wound. He was going home. Murphy took a fifty caliber slug through his thigh. A fifty caliber slug is five inches long and as thick as your thumb. His leg was barely attached to his body. Medics loaded them both onto the Medivac. It had barely lifted thirty feet off the ground when Van opened up with his own fifty caliber machine gun and blew it out of the sky. The chopper flipped over and crashed, crushing Carlos and killing him. Murphy was thrown clear. I heard later that the doctors were able to save Murphy's leg, and, although it was shorter, he was able to ride his Harley again.

Machine gun McBride was the man of the hour. A Hell's Angel when drafted, he was the platoon's lead machine gunner. Over and over again, McBride stood up in the midst of withering fire and blasted away with his M60, screaming, "More ammo; more ammo!" McBride was the only soldier I knew who had a ponytail streaming behind his helmet, and it was not his. Meanwhile, the Monitors were having a huge impact. They moved up the wood line two hundred meters and suppressed some of the enemy fire.

Charlie Nelson, a Navajo Indian warrior, stood only about five feet tall. He had not been allowed to go out on patrol because of his height and all the water we had to cross, so Charlie had become the Company mailman. He had gained some weight living on the barracks boat. The Viet Cong shot him through his newly-acquired double chin and in the leg. Charlie, who wanted so much to fight, was going home after one mission.

Meanwhile, over at what remained of A Company, soldiers valiantly attempted to survive. No reinforcements had been brought in as the gunships strafed the wood lines where the Viet Cong were dug in. Seven gunships had been shot out of the sky. Never in anyone's memory had such intense firepower been brought to bear by the so-called incompetent Viet Cong.

Van was very proud of his men. Every time a soldier moved, intense fire followed. More than three-quarters of the day was gone, and A Company was still on its own. The survivors fashioned tourniquets as best they could for the seriously wounded. Dehydration was becoming a huge problem—the result of one-hundred-degree heat, 100 percent humidity, and fighting an entrenched enemy, all with no water. Even if the survivors of A Company had water, they could not get to it as every movement attracted VC fire.

The unwounded survivors, about twenty-five in number, attempted to form a perimeter and tend to the wounded, about another twenty-five, scattered here and there. With nightfall an hour away, reinforcements still hadn't been able to enter the kill zone due to heavy enemy fire even though Charlie Company was no more than three hundred meters away.

Eric had been in and out of consciousness for the better part of eight hours after being wounded in the thigh at the beginning of the ambush. Someone had bandaged his wound and applied a tourniquet to his leg. Dehydrated and disoriented, he came to just as darkness fell. He could hear the moans of the other wounded around him and knew his chances of surviving the night were slim. About an hour after nightfall, he decided to try to crawl to where he thought friendly lines were. Every movement was agony, but the survival instinct pushed his body forward. Inch by inch, he crawled toward salvation.

Soon he saw the tree line and movement ahead. Too dehydrated to call out, he inched forward until finally, he felt hands pulling him into the tree line. The next thing he knew, he heard Vietnamese being spoken and groaned in disbelief and horror as he felt his throat being slashed. He had crawled into the hands of the Viet Cong. His battle and his life were over.

Bob's ankle was shattered by a piece of shrapnel. Somehow, he had remained conscious throughout his day of prolonged agony. Bob also realized that no aid would be coming to the survivors of A Company until morning. He had managed to retain his M-16 somehow and decided to lie where he was until help arrived. He heard Viet Cong roaming the battlefield, recovering weapons and finishing off the wounded. He felt a bayonet probe his body and then pierce his thigh, but he uttered not a sound. The Viet Cong confiscated his weapon and moved on. He passed out from fear

36

and pain. When he awoke several hours later, he decided the only thing he could do was to stay where he was and wait for help to arrive. He began to pray for the first time since he was a child.

Owen somehow remained unscathed during the battle, though as darkness approached, he was weak from fear and lack of water. About an hour after dark, he heard the cries of the wounded being assassinated by the Viet Cong. Through the course of this horrible day, he had decided on a course of action that would allow him to survive if no help came by darkness. A small stream with numerous reeds ran nearby. Owen cut a two-foot length of hollow reed and submerged himself in the water, where he quickly learned to breathe through the straw. Anything to survive.

Chuck was wounded several times and, due to loss of blood and dehydration, was delirious. He was convinced that aid was on the way even as nightfall arrived. He had numerous imaginary conversations with his fiancée, parents, and friends. He prayed for help. That help arrived in the form of a Viet Cong clothed in black with a bloody dagger. In the final greeting of his short life, Chuck mistook him for an American and welcomed him with open arms.

Ronnie could not believe what had occurred in just one day. An entire infantry company of the mighty United States Army had been wiped out by a rag-tag bunch of pajama-clad insurgents. Helicopters had been shot out of the sky, Medivacs decimated, fellow soldiers bled to death all around him, and yet Ronnie was unharmed. A coward at heart, he made no move to aid any of his fellow wounded soldiers and did not fire a single round the entire day. He realized no aid would be in the offing until daylight and barricaded himself behind a dike, ready to defend himself at all costs. No movement was good movement. Ronnie survived the night and waited to be rescued.

Van had his troops resupplied. He had plans for the coming day. He instructed 25 percent of his troops eat and rest in the local tunnels and rotated them as allowed. His day could not have been more successful. Although most of his efforts had been directed toward annihilating A Company, he received hourly reports on the attack on Charlie Company and realized that, although Charlie

Company had not been as viciously mauled as A Company, Charlie Company too had been beat up unmercifully.

Van had drawn four aces, and the Americans had no pairs. After nightfall, Van sent assassin squads into the kill zone to finish off the remains of A Company and confiscate all the weapons and supplies possible. Stripped down to basic black pajamas and carrying only daggers, the assassins roamed the kill zone at will carrying out their mission. These men had been trained to move quietly in the dark and were experts in knife fighting. None had any sympathy for the trapped Americans, having lost mothers and sisters, fathers and brothers to American aggression. They snuck soundlessly into the kill zone, picking up weapons, ammo, and supplies as they went. When they found wounded American troops, they made sure that their lives were ended. Van's men had come to respect the fighting men of the Riverine force, but realized this was a fight to the death. A Company had to be totally annihilated.

The survivors of A Company that had formed a perimeter were exhausted. Lack of water and food, as well as the overwhelming reality of the disaster that had befallen them, had left them completely numb. They took one-hour shifts of guard duty and listened to their fallen comrades being slaughtered where they lay. With very limited ammo, they could do nothing. They spent most of the night throwing back grenades lobbed into the perimeter. The survivors felt like Jesus Christ on the cross. Why had their country and comrades abandoned them? These men had only survived because of adrenalin and discipline.

Only two hundred meters away in C Company, we could also hear our fellow comrades' screams for help throughout the night. There was nothing we could do either. The Navy flotilla continuously supplied us throughout the night, and thus we had food, water, and, most importantly, ammo. Our wounded and dead had been evacuated as the supply boats returned to the barracks boat. Charlie Company was preparing for an all-out assault as soon as daylight arrived. We burned with a need to avenge our brothers on the Viet Cong. Exhausted, we ran on pure adrenaline.

We received intermittent sniper and mortar fire throughout the night—harassment fire, basically, but it served to let us know that the Viet Cong were still there. Usually the Viet Cong disappeared into the night.

An hour before dawn, word came down that there would be a full-frontal assault against the tree line separating us from the survivors of A Company. I felt the cold vibration of sheer terror move along my spine. Finally, fifteen minutes before we were to attack, the word came to stand down. We suddenly heard the roar of jet aircraft in the distance. The command radio and telephone operators were relaying coordinates of the surviving troops, and Bravo Company was being brought in to relieve what was left of A Company.

I couldn't help but wonder why this had not done the night before. The jets screamed in and dropped napalm in the tree lines surrounding the remains of Charlie Company and A Company. Help had finally arrived. We could hear horrible screams from every area of the enemy's positions. The survivors of A Company let out cheers as they watched the massive firepower being brought to bear on the enemy. After an hour of heavy bombardment by the jets, the order came down to saddle up. The ground assault on enemy positions had begun.

When Van heard the sound of the enemy planes approaching in the distance, he ordered his troops to hunker down in the various tunnels honeycombing the area and sent word to the troops surrounding Charlie Company to do the same. The Viet Cong had plenty of ammunition and supplies, and their dead and wounded had been moved out during the night.

The heat and incessant bombing were almost unbearable in the tunnels, and Van thought he would go mad. But he had been through this before and knew it couldn't go on forever. He prepared his troops to kill more Americans. Once the air attack was over, he saw and heard that the American troops had been resupplied and reinforced and were forcing enemy troops out of their positions around Charlie Company and toward his position. He decided it was time to withdraw his troops to fight another day. All in all, the last two days had been the most successful of Van's short life.

As I and my fellow troopers gained the upper hand on the enemy, I could see over into the area where the remains of A

Company were strewn over a wide area. There was little movement. Our jets pounded the wood line, and one Viet Cong attempted to shoot down a jet with his old M1 carbine. I thought, "After all the Viet Cong have been through and after losing so many men, how can I expect to defeat an enemy who will not give up? Impossible." As Charlie Company moved through the wood line, we saw numerous blood trails—but no bodies. I felt as if I was living in a Twilight Zone.

We slowly worked our way toward where the remaining survivors of A Company huddle in their makeshift perimeter. Bodies, weapons, and gear lay everywhere. Every once in a while, a survivor was miraculously found and aid rendered. The surviving troopers were zombies, all suffering from the thousand-mile stare that sees nothing. Some jokingly ask, "Where you guys been? The party's over."

The enemy had left few bodies and far fewer wounded. It was as if they had all been ghosts. By the time it was all over, A Company had eighty-five soldiers killed, forty-five wounded, and only twenty uninjured physically. In Charlie Company, we had twenty killed and forty wounded. All the survivors would be mentally scarred the rest of their lives, all because of one incompetent captain. The battalion would have had casualties, but nowhere near what transpired had better decisions been made.

What remained of the battalion returned to the barracks ship. The most poignant scene occurred on the floating dock, where the battalion cleaned up after their patrols and piled stacks upon stacks of soldiers' gear high to wait for cleanup crews. The only things that could not be reclaimed were the human lives lost. Approximately one hundred "Sorry to inform you of the death of your son or husband" letters were in the process of being hand delivered. The actions of A Company were being reviewed, and the only action the battalion could take was to remove the captain so that he could not endanger any more lives.

The discarded equipment on the dock belied the stories the men of the battalion had heard about the incompetence of the Viet Cong as a fighting machine. The men were allowed four days off to recharge their batteries. I felt sorry for the replacements coming out of the states after just sixteen weeks of training. They were being placed in A Company, which had just been wiped off the face of the earth. The "old timers" gave a cold shoulder to the replacements after witnessing the deaths of their buddies. What they didn't realize was that this coldness would accompany them into civilian life, never again allowing them normal human emotions.

The most prominent symbol of the debacle was the fleet of aluminum motor boats floating next to the dock. They had been responsible for the deaths of ten C Company soldiers. During the middle of the night, three troopers snuck among the boats after informing the guards of their intentions and destroyed them with hand grenades. No investigation was forthcoming.

The captain of A Company was very antagonistic to the criticism being heaped on him by the High Command and the survivors of the attack. In his mind, there was a higher concentration of Viet Cong in his area of operations than Charlie Company had, and the ambush was sprung on A Company before Charlie Company moved into its area of operations. Thus, in his mind, he was a victim of circumstances, as were his men. The captain of A Company had a lot in common with Custer, with one big difference: At least Custer had the grace to die with his men.

CHAPTER

7

The men of Charlie Company had four days to regroup on the barracks ship and digest the disaster that had befallen their battalion. In the course of conversation, I found it strange how the Viet Cong knew exactly where both A Company and C Company were going to land that day. Could it be that the battle plan had been passed on to the Viet Cong by someone high up in the South Vietnamese Army? I also wondered if the battalion had been set up like sacrificial lambs in order to draw the Viet Cong into a major battle so that the our superior air power and Monitors could bring in a higher body count.

The word was that the battle was being promoted as a major Allied victory with hundreds of Viet Cong being eliminated, even though the casualty toll to the Allied forces was unacceptable. The idea that I was cannon fodder had been growing in my mind for a long time. This thought was so repugnant to my mind that I felt I may as well have committed suicide. After a while, my attitude improved as I realized that I had survived six months of combat whereas many had not. I knew that this was a result of serendipity more than skill, but still—it made me a survivor.

Word filtered down that anyone with one year in the military could extend his enlistment by two years and be transferred off the line into a noncombat job. This was a very attractive prospect, but two years was a very long time to a twenty-one-year-old. However, six more months in combat loomed almost as a death sentence. I decided the odds were too high against me and searched out the re-enlistment officer.

Unfortunately, he was on R&R and wouldn't return until after the next patrol. I resigned myself to one more patrol. The Company was going back into the Rung Sat (Forest of the Assassins), a salt-water cypress swamp, to seek out arms caches. We had been there before. Mud, leeches, crocodiles, exhaustion, heat, humidity, booby traps, rain, and Viet Cong awaited.

C Company was dropped off at 7:00 am. Lt. Jones, the executive officer, was in command of the operation. A hard-charging individual whose normal duties as executive officer were to handle resupply, replacements, and logistics, Jones had never been in combat and was walking on water in his new role as Company Commander. The company commander.

We patrolled until noon and broke for a lunch of C rations, having only moved five hundred meters in four hours due to rough terrain. Soon after resuming patrol, we discovered a Viet Cong base camp. Rice was still warm in the pot, so we knew the Viet Cong were nearby. A large arms cache surrounded by booby traps was discovered. Lt. Jones came forward before the demolition experts arrived on scene and declared that he would disarm the booby trap himself. His command group tried to dissuade him from such action, but he was headstrong. As he leaned over the first booby trap, he tripped it and it exploded in his face. He died immediately—twenty-three years old, impaled on the spear of war and stupidity.

Our platoon stayed there over night, removing the arms cache after demolitions experts disarmed the booby traps. We were hoping the Viet Cong would return, but they weren't that stupid. We moved out cautiously the next morning, knowing that we were probably under constant surveillance. We were to be picked up and returned to the barracks ship at 2:00 pm. due to being under strength. The day was uneventful, giving me plenty of time to think about the future. It had become quite obvious that my number was going to come up sooner or later. The events of the last few days had reinforced the thought that investing an extra two years in the military would be worth avoiding serious injury or death, but I still wasn't convinced it was the right move for me. The platoon flew to a forward artillery base near Highway 1 and pulled security for a week.

Each morning a squad of ten men left the artillery base at 7:00 am. and cleared the two-mile stretch of dirt road leading from Highway 1. When my squad's turn came, we had a new leader who thought he knew it all, fresh from the states. About half way through clearing the road, the squad leader leaned over and revealed a length of demo wire stretched across the track. He looked at it, dropped it, and continued on. I thought it should've been obvious that the wire was there for a reason and its source should be investigated, but the sergeant was in charge and I didn't question him.

The squad returned to the artillery base without incident, and no report was made of the suspicious wire. The next morning at about 0730, I heard an explosion and a great deal of automatic weapons fire. The squad clearing the access road had been ambushed. The platoon rushed out to aid the beleaguered men and found three dead, three wounded, and the remainder in shock.

One of the men had been killed in the very spot I had been standing when the sergeant spotted the wire. I knew that in his heart, the sergeant had probably saved my life by not examining the wire more closely, but I also knew that through the sergeant's stupidity, other men had been wounded and killed. Such were the vagaries of life and death. I had finally come to the conclusion that I was playing with a loaded deck and that the two-year extension was worth it. However, instead of heading back to the boats, our company had a three-day search and destroy mission. I couldn't see the reenlistment officer until it was over.

After two days of slogging through mud and rice paddies with no action, my squad was assigned a ten-man lookout post about one hundred meters from the company perimeter. Since eight of the ten men were new in country, I and the other veteran took the later watches. The new men tended to fall asleep. Around 2200, one of the rookies woke me and informed me that a patrol of ten men had just walked through within fifteen feet carrying their weapons by the barrel as the ARVN did, so they hadn't fired on them. Since the area the company was in was a kill zone, anything that moved at night was presumed to be Viet Cong. Immediately fully awake, I took control of the machine gun and the plungers for the claymore mines.

The moon came up around midnight, and I saw a figure come out of the wood line one hundred meters out heading straight at me. I thought he might be the point man of the Viet Cong patrol that passed earlier and didn't want to reveal our position. Before I knew it, the figure was directly in front of me and I tackled him. The figure came down on me as if he had a weapon, and I thought, "I really screwed up this time!" As it turned out, the Viet Cong's hand had been blown off in a previous engagement. He needed a doctor.

I thought I would be a hero for capturing a live Viet Cong who might provide information about enemy activity. Upon returning to base camp, I was instead ridiculed by many of my fellow soldiers for not having tortured and killed my captive. This terrified me more than anything I had encountered yet. All I could think was that these soldiers were back on the block in New York, Pittsburgh, Chicago, or some small farm community just a year previously living as normal, civilized American teenagers, and after being exposed to combat, the majority had reverted to barbarians. I was now adamant about extending for two years.

CHAPTER

8

Tuyen was ready to take on her assignment to My Tho. During the previous months, she'd evolved into a sophisticated, well mannered, beautiful young woman schooled in the ways of espionage. Colonel Khan came across Tuyen when she first arrived in Saigon. He found her obvious beauty and her dedication to the cause equally appealing. She was quite naive as to the ways of a cosmopolitan city, but she was willing to learn. Several matronly teachers, knowledgeable in manners, language, and social etiquette, imparted their wisdom to her. Her Communist brainwashing having already been accomplished by Van, she devoted all her time to becoming a woman of the world.

That was all accomplished within six months—and then the real training began. Tuyen was schooled in using her feminine wiles to seduce United States servicemen. She learned what they like, which was not hard to do, since they were all lonely and far from home. She was put through a so-called training course run by professional prostitutes of Saigon to learn to perform sexual acts without emotion and eliminate love from her emotions. Tuyen held within her heart her love for Van exclusively.

Colonel Khan kept track of her progress and was well pleased. Once Tuyen's training was over, Colonel Khan had her assigned to him as his secretary, supposedly to further her knowledge of Communist theory. As a result, she and Colonel Khan spent many lunches together and, eventually, every evening as well. Soon their relationship became sexual, with the fifty-year-old Colonel Khan devoting all his repressed love to her and her servicing Colonel Khan as she would an American Soldier.

Tuyen kept her love for Van from Colonel Khan, and through him, she was able to get information about Van. In return for bestowing her sexual attributes on Colonel Khan, she received special treatment. Colonel Khan had become the first focus of her new found abilities. They spent many nights together in Saigon, and through him, she heard about Van's tremendous success against the Riverine force at Ap Bac. She thanked all the gods she prayed to for Van's safety and asked them for advice in her relationship with Colonel Khan. Tuyen came to the conclusion that this sexual relationship would not go against her devotion to Van, as that relationship did not preclude a nonemotional sexual relationship.

Colonel Khan was married to his childhood sweetheart and was the father of two teenage boys who fought with the Viet Cong at Dak To in the central highlands, where a tremendous battle was taking place with the American Fourth Infantry Division. Colonel Khan wished he were fighting alongside his sons, but once his tryst with Tuyen materialized, he dedicated himself to the blossoming of their relationship. He saw his family maybe twice a year and described the relationship to Tuyen as long-suffering on all sides.

Colonel Khan had known war his entire life. He arrived in the Mekong Delta twenty years prior as a raw recruiting officer with the theory being that it would be much easier for a recruiting officer with no local ties to indoctrinate and win over the local populace to the beliefs of Communism. He had accomplished much over the years. The Mekong Delta became a sanctuary for the Viet Cong, and although the local population knew little about

Communist theory, they did know that it was to their advantage to have someone win the war, as the farmers were being taxed by both sides.

The control of the Mekong Delta by Colonel Khan lessened as the Riverine force became established in the area, making his job much more difficult. At one time, he had control over 75 percent of the Delta. But the incursion of the "River Rats" hurt his control of the population and greatly reduced the supply of arms available to his forces. His relationship with his wife became more distant each year, and although his feelings for his family were still strong, his love for his wife had gradually transformed into a brotherly affection.

Tuyen didn't live with the Colonel; that would have been too scandalous. But he made sure she was well taken care of. Van was one of his subordinates in the field and never left his men. Colonel Khan was unaware of Tuyen's relationship with Van and thought nothing of her request to be assigned to the My Tho district, where much fighting was in progress. The assignment placed Tuyen in the vicinity of Van's area of operations while putting her in the perfect position to have a great deal of contact with American soldiers, increasing her ability to gather intelligence. She had an emotional farewell with Colonel Khan—the emotion his alone. He indicated that there would be a large operation at the beginning of 1968, and after that, he promised, he would arrange for them to be together forever.

Tuyen moved to My Tho and began working in the main PX. She had never seen so many products at such cheap prices, all subsidized by the American taxpayer. Every G.I. assigned to the My Tho district had to shop at the PX. It took her several weeks to become acquainted with the procedures, but she was a fast learner. She roomed with two other girls. Neither were politically oriented but were simply looking for a suitable G.I. to seduce and marry so they could live happily ever after in the United States.

Slowly but surely, Tuyen learned to spot soldiers who were assigned to the intelligence units by their shoulder patches and began to pay them special attention. Each week she was introduced to more of the Communist cadre, and was eventually assigned to

Madame Long, a lady of great worldliness and many wealthy contacts. She would be a crucial contact when the time came to entertain a G.I.

Madame Long had been part of the Communist movement since the Japanese kicked out the French in 1942, and she relocated to the Mekong Delta after Ho Chi Minh drove out the French in 1952. She hated the Allied forces with a passion, having lost her entire family to the bombs of World War II and been imprisoned and tortured herself. As Tuyen's major contact, Madame Long was able to spend a lot of time with her further refining her capabilities. The greatest lesson Madame Long could impart to her was the lesson of patience. "For all things come to those who wait," she said.

CHAPTER
9

Van had been in Cambodia for over a month. The American forces foolishly respected Cambodian neutrality, and, as a result, the Viet Cong had been stockpiling weapons, recruiting new troops, retraining existing troops, and generally becoming more professional in the art of war. As a result of his successes against the Ninth Infantry Division Mobile Riverine force in the Mekong Delta, Van had been placed in charge of the troops assembled in Cambodia and increased in rank to Lt. Colonel. He was aware of Tuyen's activities in My Tho and longed to see her. She was the only weakness in his strict human armor.

Van answered directly to Colonel Khan, acting as his eyes and ears in Cambodia. The more trained personnel Colonel Khan had in the Mekong Delta and Cambodia, the greater their chance of success when the major attack occurred. The High Command in Hanoi was convinced that once the Communist forces exhibited a force of power in South Vietnam, the majority of the population would revolt against the corrupt Saigon government and join the Communist ranks.

Thousands of bus boys, bartenders, bar girls, barbers, and rickshaw drivers all over South Vietnam provided the Communists with American base blueprints, troop movements, and supply and ammunition depot locations. All were in sympathy with the movement, believing that their lives would improve under a Communist takeover. Recruiting was going so well that Van was able to pick and choose the best available cadre to become professional soldiers. Those less capable would be used as ammo bearers and supply personnel.

The majority of Communist sympathizers had lost family and friends to the imperialist forces and burned with the need to eliminate the Saigon government and remove American forces and their allies from Vietnam. The goal was to create a Vietnamese country governed by the Vietnamese and free of the influence of any foreign power. The idea was that Vietnam would be devoted to the concept of one for all and all for one. Individual life paled in comparison to the common good. All were willing to sacrifice their lives in order to establish a united Vietnam.

Colonel Khan continued his preparations for the overthrow of the Saigon government. His intelligence contacts with the ARVN forces extended all the way up to the top generals. This was how the Viet Cong were able to know when and where the Mobile Riverine force would disembark on June 19 and practically annihilate A Company. These generals were well paid for the intelligence, and all had Swiss bank accounts. Capitalism permeated their attitude. Dying for the cause was for the masses. All the Generals had residences outside the country, and all had made arrangements to have their families or mistresses whisked there when the Communists succeeded. They all paid homage to the god of gold.

Colonel Khan was no different. As monies flowed to his bank accounts to pay off the ARVN generals, Colonel Khan bled off his fair share, which was transferred to his own Swiss bank account. Men of power who are corrupt differ little in their need for material wealth. Morality and social conscience be damned. Colonel Khan maintained his appearance of revolutionary zeal amongst his comrades in arms but was gradually setting himself up for a life of opulence in a foreign country. He cared not if he ever saw his wife again, and as his sons were grown and had their own moral convictions, their lives were of no concern to him. He revealed a little of his plans for the future to Tuyen, only saying that he foresaw a safe, luxurious future, hopefully together.

He continued his preparations for the coming attack. He had fifty thousand troops under his command and another ten thousand informants feeding information through his intelligence apparatus. This never-ending flow of information about American and ARVN troop movements and plans allowed him to continually harass the allied troops, causing maximum casualties through booby traps and snipers. He was also able to avoid any major battles, resulting in minimal casualties on his side. Through Van, Colonel Khan used the Cambodian sanctuary to his best advantage.

Colonel Khan could not have been in a more commanding position. He continued to oversee the review of troop training and stockpiling of weapons and supplies using the disguise of a Buddhist monk who traveled the countryside giving solace to the peasantry. This allowed him to make numerous journeys to My Tho to keep an eye on Tuyen and experience the joys of their relationship. He was able to accomplish this with the aid of Madame Long, who provided him with safe haven and a secluded villa.

During these interludes with Tuyen, he reiterated to her that there was a major offensive planned for early 1968 and explained that the more intelligence she could glean from the Americans, the better. He also hinted that no matter which side was victorious, he would be leaving the country to retire to a life of luxury and had arranged for Tuyen to accompany him. She greeted this news outwardly with joy, but inwardly, she realized she must inform Van of the colonel's plan for escape as soon as possible so she could remain with Van forever.

Colonel Khan became increasingly dependent on Van to be his eyes and ears in the field while he concentrated on recruitment and intelligence operations. The colonel was an expert on anticipating the enemy's movements and was certainly helped by the numerous spies in both the ARVN organization and the civilian population. Orders came from Hanoi to prepare for a major offensive to be conducted during the TET religious holidays in late January 1968. There were to be major diversionary attacks at Khe San near the DMZ and at Dak To in the central highlands in an attempt to draw allied forces to these areas and lull the allied command into a sense of security in the rest of the country.

CHAPTER

10

I made my way to the recruiting officer's quarters. I had already made peace with my conscience over abandoning my buddies, and, since so few were left, I had little trouble extending the two years in order to get out of combat. My conversation with the recruiter was short and sweet. In exchange for the extra two years' service, I was to be removed from combat and would return to the United States on the date I was supposed to.

In the meantime, I had my choice of several operational assignments at offices in Vietnam, most of which entailed boring jobs. The one exception was an assignment to My Tho in the Mekong Delta, which would automatically raise my rank to E-5 and place me in a clerk's position in the intelligence office. This would allow me to keep track of my old unit while performing a job of some interest. I had no problem choosing.

Upon arrival in My Tho, I reported immediately to my assigned office. I was one of three clerks, all of the same rank, whose job it was to process reports from the field concerning intelligence and counter insurgent measures. I found the work fascinating and engrossing. I was in the know about what was going on and soon received a higher security clearance. I spent my off-duty hours writing letters home and counting the days until my return.

I avoided the bars and drug dens of My Tho at night. Having seen several of my coworkers slip into the routine of getting high every night due to boredom, I realized how easy it was to fall prey to that kind of habit. My one bad habit was hanging around the PX drooling over the myriad items available to those with money and envisioning ownership of all the items I desired. I could even buy a car there.

This new life was a far cry from slogging around the muddy, leech-infected environs of the Mekong Delta. I saved every penny I could with the aim of having a stake when I returned home. My job granted me increased responsibility every week as other clerks returned home. I transcribed all the reports emanating from Long Range Recon forays sent into Cambodia to check on the Viet Cong buildup there. All of these forays involved the Parrots Peak area, where it was obvious the Viet Cong were building up a force to make a major attack. Although illegal, bombings were constantly directed into this area, which resulted in a curtailment of the munitions buildup and forced the Viet Cong to move more of their operations underground.

United States combat fatalities had fallen as the majority of Viet Cong personnel spent their time stockpiling munitions and training for the major push against the allied forces. As I kept track of enemy troop buildup and transcribed SOG (Special Operations Group) after-action reports, I stood in awe of their bravery and envious of their experiences yet thankful that it was their job and not mine—they suffered 75 percent casualty rates.

I was also privy to CIA prisoner interrogation reports, and the techniques used in these interrogations shocked me. In one case in particular, CIA agents transporting two Viet Cong prisoners to My Tho from the Parrots Peak area by helicopter dangled one of the prisoners out the door of the chopper and demanded information on troop concentrations and movement. They finally dropped the untalkative Viet Cong from a height of five hundred feet into the jungle. Immediately, the other prisoner became very talkative. The information the CIA agents received was of questionable quality, given the interrogation techniques, but the practice happened more than once. I didn't condone the practice but chose to ignore it as long as it produced results. Morality be damned.

After one month, I rose in the hierarchy of the office of the internal intelligence community. The officers involved in intelligence gathering and spy mongering realized that any reports needed quickly and error free should be requested of me. As a result, my work load increased, my grasp of the Viet Cong organizational system improved, and I realized that I really enjoyed what I was doing. Sometimes I heard and saw things I wished I had not. The intelligence unit and their CIA counterpart stopped at nothing to extract information from their prisoners. The Geneva Conventions were nonexistent in the Mekong Delta. It became apparent to me that the Communists were up to something big— the question was when.

CHAPTER
11

I looked forward to my next rendezvous with Tuyen, which wasn't scheduled for several days. I buried myself in work and learned just how dirty a business the intelligence game was. In order for field personnel to accomplish their objectives of intelligence gathering, the Geneva Conventions did not apply. No one ever gave out information willingly on either side, and the enemy was never known to leave wounded or captured soldiers alive.

The human race quickly returns to barbarism once the veneer of civilization has been removed. Water torture was a common tactic and very effective. Hose beatings, red ant attacks, and sleep deprivation were common tactics in the field. Upon arrival at intelligence headquarters, more civilized tactics were put into play. Starvation, dehydration, and brainwashing were all used effectively. The last resort was to threaten the prisoner with turning him over to ARVN interrogators who understood the oriental mind and resorted to the most bestial applications of torture known to man. I realized that these tactics were necessary and acceptable in the cause of obtaining information. Anything the Allied forces could learn that contributed to the saving of Allied lives was condoned.

Strangely, I missed my forays into the field—the rush of adrenalin brought by combat—and found myself reaching complacency at my desk-bound job. Since I had gained the personal trust of both the officers and enlisted men in my compound, I was allowed to sit in on debriefings of field troops, where I found myself envying them for their adventures. These men were SOG detachments consisting of Green Berets, Seals, and Ranger personnel who had been selected for covert operations into Viet Cong and sanctuaries in Cambodia to assess troop strengths and activities. Only the best of the best were chosen, as all members of the elite troops involved desired to go on these missions.

With an attrition rate of 70 percent, many if not all of those who wished to participate eventually did. They operated as four- to six-man teams, and many times, an entire team never returned. The biggest problem with team success was that they had to operate as an integrated unit, and, with the ever-present lack of personnel, that became increasingly difficult.

Because the teams acted covertly, killed members were listed as missing in action, with some kind of legitimate story made up to account for their deaths. All conflicts were with enemy forces that vastly outnumbered the four-man teams—rarely was a wounded SOG member rescued. Once a team was discovered, it was a fight to the death. Their job was to gather information, assess enemy troop strengths, and direct air strikes on enemy training camps and supply depots. The operational policy was aimed at eliminating the enemy's ability to wage war.

At first the Communists in Cambodia were content to hide their staging areas under the dense jungle canopy. As the incursion of SOG teams increased and staging areas increasingly came under attack by high-altitude B-52 air strikes, the Communists became adept at hiding their troops and supplies underground or in mountain caves. Van required more and more coolie labor in order to enlarge existing tunnels and obtained these forces from the native Cambodian population. This conscription wasn't voluntary but was took place with full knowledge of the Cambodian government. These Cambodian conscripts were forced into slave labor by realistic threats to their families. Thus the SOG's effectiveness waned as time went on.

As I became increasingly bored with my mentally stimulating but ultimately mundane—compared to the six months of adrenaline rush I had experienced in combat—intelligence job, I devised a plan to accompany an SOG team on a mission into Cambodia.

The first order of business was to exhibit my physical readiness to engage in such an operation. I began a routine of physical training that would qualify me for the extremes of an SOG operation, and I made sure the SOG teams were aware of my efforts. My fellow clerks made fun of my ambition. Of course, most of them had become drug addicts and alcoholics after a few short weeks behind the desk, and their first order of business every morning was to vomit and have a cigarette.

After a few weeks of my training regimen, I was invited to join the SOG teams in their day-to-day physical training when they weren't on missions. Each training session increased my camaraderie with the men of SOG, and I lived and died with them when their missions succeeded—or, in a worst-case scenario, when the team disappeared.

I made it known to SOG team members that I was very envious of their accomplishments and that I was quite capable as a radio and telephone operator (RTO). I also made my superior officer aware of my desire to participate in an SOG ground operation, whereupon I was instantly rebuffed. I expected this but also knew that as manpower availability was reduced, my chance would come. My motivations were fourfold: I missed the adrenaline rush of combat, I was enamored of the four- to six-man operating units of the SOG teams as opposed to the platoon- and company-size operations I was used to, I felt useless as a clerk, and I had a need within me to prove to myself that I was not a coward.

During the summer of 1967, the SOG teams experienced terrible losses. Of the twenty four-man teams operating out of My Tho, six did not return while the rest lost between 25 and 50 percent of their men. Replacements were hard to come by because of increased NVA infiltration into Dak To in the central highlands and Khe San on the DMZ. I repeatedly heard SOG team members and officers complain about the lack of qualified personnel and the need for more SOG teams to spy on the Communists in Cambodia. The Communist numbers in that area were increasing, and all indications were that a major offensive was in the offing.

All SOG teams were operating on a one-day rest break between missions as opposed to the normal three days. All personnel knew that despite the physical determination of the SOG personnel, the mental stress was unbearable. Soon, only eight teams were operational—far below what was needed.

I approached the commander of the SOG forces at My Tho and volunteered for the next mission into Cambodia. Aware of my interfacing with the SOG teams physically and mentally, and desperately in need of an experienced RTO, the SOG team commander agreed to approach my superior officer and request my assignment to an SOG team for one operation.

My commanding officer was aghast at the idea, mainly because he was a kiss-ass who didn't want anyone rocking his boat. When the SOG commander proposed issuing orders assigning me to the SOG team temporarily, my commanding officer readily agreed, as this relieved him of any responsibility. He was also outranked.

I was immediately taken to the SOG compound in My Tho and introduced to the SOG team I would be working with. I was aware that this unit was very secretive about individual members' true identities for several reasons. First, if anyone was captured, the less they knew about other members, the better. Familiarity bred contempt, and the less anyone knew about his teammates, the easier it was to perform as commandos. Last but not least, I was a newbie and had to prove myself to the other members of the team before I could gain their respect.

The other members of the team were introduced as Sal, Frankie, and Doug. I had worked out with Sal and Frankie and thus had a limited rapport with them, but Doug had just shipped in from the central highlands and thus was in a way a newbie himself.

Sal, the team leader, came to the team from a SEAL detachment. He'd served three tours in the Mekong Delta and knew it like the back of his hand. Sal had made ten drops into Cambodia and was respected for only losing one fellow team member and having only two wounded team members.

Frankie had been with the SOG teams in My Tho for more than three months and was an expert tracker. This was his second tour, and he was formerly a Long Range Recon member.

Doug was on his third tour and came from a Green Beret unit in the central highlands. His demeanor was that of a cold, efficient killer, and all any one knew about him came from his indication that the Green Berets never let any prisoners survive and were experts at extracting information.

Our team had a pre-op review meeting, went over the proposed insertion site, and was informed that there had been intelligence from recon flights of increased enemy activity in the area. We were definitely being dropped into Cambodia, and into an area where no allied forces had ever operated.

I felt the scream of fear develop in my guts but also experienced the first jolt of adrenaline rush in my veins in some time. Somehow I craved more.

The Hueys would take off at 0600 from My Tho and insert the team after a thirty-minute flight. It was emphasized to us that we would be operating in an area off limits to allied troops and that the focus of our mission was intelligence gathering, not combat. If we performed our mission properly, we would return to base with no shots fired. If any member of the team was captured, there would be no acknowledgment of their being part of the Allied forces, and each man would be on his own. I was further instructed as to radio operations of the SOG team and given several radio frequencies to call in air strikes, and, most importantly, extraction forces. We retreated to the mess hall for a final steak dinner and early sack out in order to wake up at 0500 for breakfast and the distribution of munitions.

I lay awake for some time pondering my decision to reenter the field of combat. Why, I wondered, would I volunteer for such a dangerous mission when I had already agreed to spend two more years of my life in the military in order to avoid combat? My conclusion was that I had to prove to myself that I was not a coward, and an equal motivator was my need for the adrenaline rush of combat.

At 0500, we were awakened for breakfast. Afterward we were issued three days' rations, thirty clips of M-16 ammo, five grenades, a claymore mine, and three canteens of water. I was also issued my radio. All members carried a smoke grenade to indicate their position for extraction. It was reiterated that our mission was never to engage the enemy, only gather intelligence.

Radio contact would be kept to a minimum. With the most experience as an SOG team member, Sal was appointed team leader. He made it clear that he would brook no disagreements among the team members. He treated us as equals among professionals and made it clear that no one on the team outranked anyone else, regardless of experience or rank. Frank had three tours of experience with the SOG teams in My Tho and had experienced the stark terror of team members being lost in the jungles of Cambodia. He was one of those guys who thrived under pressure.

At 0600 we boarded the helicopter. For the thirty-minute flight, the helicopter flew at high altitude to evade enemy detection. The weather had cleared. Suddenly, the Huey dove down to tree level and settled into a clearing measuring one hundred meters square. The team immediately exited our bird of destiny and disappeared into the jungle. Silence enveloped us.

After pushing fifty meters into the heavy jungle foliage, Sal signaled a halt to listen for enemy presence. We remained silent for two hours, absorbing the sounds of the jungle. There was no sign reading "Phnom Penh, Cambodia: 50 miles," but we were all very aware that we were in Cambodia. Finally, after detecting no enemy presence, we pressed on through the jungle until we come upon a heavily used trail leading off to the south. Sal immediately sent Frank and Doug on a recon mission, and they quickly returned indicating the trail was heavily traveled, but there was no sign of enemy troops.

The team commenced at a slow pace until dusk, when we melted into the jungle and became invisible until dawn. It was my responsibility to send the coordinates of our location back to My Tho in case we were discovered during the night. I also had to press the "send" key every three hours to inform the SOG command that we were still undetected.

This didn't allow for a lot of sleep. One man was on guard every two hours. The rest of us chowed down and settled into a precarious slumber. About midnight, I heard sounds coming from the trail five meters from us. Everyone awoke immediately. For a period of thirty minutes, we could hear enemy troops and supplies moving along the trail. When Sal was sure that all was clear, he signaled the team to move forward slowly so as not to bump into the enemy column. We did this in order to make sure our team would be able to follow the column to its final destination. They were heading south to what appeared to be some kind of rendezvous. We slowly crept through the jungle and, after about an hour, detected a large force about fifty meters away.

Doug was sent on recon and quickly returned with a report that sent shivers up my spine. We had discovered a major enemy supply and training area in Cambodia that was undetectable from the air. Sal decided to put the team to ground until daylight, when we would commence with a further recon of the area. No one slept the rest of the night. When dawn came, Sal sent Doug on a second recon mission. He returned an hour later and indicated through sign language that we had stumbled upon a major staging area for troops and supplies in Cambodia. The area had a constant flow of activity and large entrances to huge caverns where the enemy was storing supplies and munitions. Hundreds, if not thousands, of Communist troops were in some form of training.

Our team had hit the mother load. Sal had me contact SOG command and relay the intelligence we had discovered. The team went to ground again and, during the course of the morning, observed two more caravans of supplies and munitions being delivered to the camp. About noon, I received a message to check the coordinates of the camp. B-52 strikes were being planned for the next morning, and High Command wanted to be sure they got a direct hit. After I confirmed the coordinates, the team was advised to maintain position until the next morning, when the air strikes were to commence. The team would be given thirty minutes' notice to move back through the jungle to our drop-off point for pick up.

I realized this was a very dangerous situation. It was very likely the Viet Cong had patrols out looking for us, and it was only a matter of time before they found our trail. Our team was in no position to argue, and we realized that High Command was willing to risk our lives when the air strikes were ready rather than reveal our position prematurely.

We settled in for a long night of waiting and thinking. Van was in charge of the training and supply compound we had located. He received reports of a helicopter in the area the previous day and had sent out increased recon to try and locate any allied patrol. He knew that no allied helicopter was going to stray into Cambodia without a specific reason, and all his defensive antennae were on alert.

Toward the end of the day, a patrol came in with information that a clearing had been located up the trail by which men and materials came down from North Vietnam. In this clearing were indications of American Army boot prints and of a possible drop-off of a small enemy patrol. Van bristled at this information, knowing that his location was extremely vulnerable with men and supplies out in the open due to a lack of room in the cave.

Since darkness had descended, Van decided to send out the maximum number of patrols possible at dawn. I sent in situation reports throughout the night indicating that our team hadn't moved. An hour before dawn, we readied ourselves for a quick run to the pickup point before bombs began to lay waste and destruction to the Viet Cong encampment.

As dawn approached and it became obvious that more patrols were emanating from the Viet Cong staging area, Sal decided to make a break for the pickup point prematurely. Almost immediately, we heard a Viet Cong patrol coming toward us. Our team melted into the jungle. As soon as Sal felt it was safe, we resumed our journey. Shortly thereafter, we came under attack from their rear. The Viet Cong patrol had decoyed us and were hot on our trail. We all lay down suppression fire while Sal set up two clay-more mines on the trail.

As the enemy approached, Sal detonated the mines and screams from the enemy patrol resounded throughout the jungle. This gave us time to reassemble and head for the pickup point ten minutes away. Other Viet Cong patrols had picked up the scent and were closing in. As we neared the pickup point, Doug hung back voluntarily to allow us to set up and wait for extraction.

We heard the rescue chopper in the distance, followed by a sudden scream from Doug. Then, nothing but silence. Doug had sacrificed himself for the good of the team. The rest of us continued to attack the enemy patrol with hand grenades. The chopper touched down just as Frank was struck in the chest. Sal hoisted Frank into the chopper and was himself hit while I continued to fire.

As I fell into the chopper, I realized I had been wounded in the leg. I fought for consciousness as the chopper, riddled with bullet holes, quickly headed back to My Tho. In my own daze, I heard the tremendous explosions occurring at the Viet Cong staging area in Cambodia, as well as the tremendous residual explosions of stored ammunition being ignited by low-flying jets dropping napalm.

At the site of the Viet Cong staging area, Van was in a state of shock. Many months of preparation, bringing supplies and muni-tions for the coming offensive, had gone up in smoke. Hundreds of his men had been killed or seriously wounded. Van wasn't as concerned about the men as he was about the supplies. Men could be quickly replaced, but supplies were invaluable; they took time to replace. Van vowed revenge on whoever was responsible for this debacle.

CHAPTER
12

The captain of the SOG came in at about 1000 hours to give me an after-action report. He indicated that the bombing of the supply and training facility in Cambodia appeared to have been the most important of the war with both elimination of supplies and munitions and the wiping out of hundreds, if not thousands, of Communist soldiers.

I inquired about the other members of the team and was informed that I was the only survivor. I remembered Doug being killed in Cambodia but thought the other members had survived, even if they had been wounded. The captain informed me that Frank and Sal were both seriously wounded as they entered the rescue helicopter and had died before arriving in My Tho. I could only think that I was a survivor again. The captain promised to return the next day to debrief me about what had transpired in Cambodia and ordered me to speak to no one about the classified mission.

I drifted in and out of sleep during the day and, thanks to a strong sleeping pill, slept almost until noon. After eating another huge meal, I dozed through the afternoon. I woke about 1700 to find a beautiful Vietnamese volunteer standing next to my bed.

"I am glad to see you awake," she whispered. "You have been sleeping for two days, which is good for you, but tomorrow, you must get out of bed and start to walk around in order to regain your balance. We met at the PX before you disappeared. I am Tuyen."

"I am pleased to see you again," I replied, "though not necessarily under these circumstances. What are you doing here?"

"I volunteer here at the hospital after my shift at the PX is over to help wounded soldiers such as yourself. I will get you some special dessert if you wish."

"I would appreciate that greatly. Although the food here is plentiful, sweets are in short supply."

Tuyen returned shortly with a large bowl of vanilla ice cream, which I devoured.

"Tell me about yourself and what you have been doing?" I asked.

"I was born on Th oi Son Island in the north of the Mekong Delta twenty-four years ago. My mother is still there, but my father passed away five years ago after the Viet Cong took over the island and destroyed our way of life. My father died as much from depression as from any physical ailment. I have two brothers who serve with the ARVN forces and of whom I worry all the time. After my father died, my mother sent me to wealthy relatives in Saigon, who sent me to excellent schools where I learned English. I live with three roommates who also work at the PX, and I have been in My Tho for two months." She paused before adding, "I was disappointed that you never showed up for our next meeting."

"I was called out on a special mission, which I can't discuss. I am just trying to accept the fact that I am the only survivor of the four men who were with me."

Not wishing to alarm me with too many questions, she pretended not to hear this last statement.

"Tell me about your background in the United States and how you arrived in My Tho?" Tuyen inquired.

"I come from Chicago, where everything revolves around politics and sports. My dad owns an Irish bar, my mother is a bookkeeper, and I have one sister. I hope to return and become a police officer. I fooled around at college, flunked out, and was quickly drafted. My unit was assigned to the Mekong Delta and has been involved in many battles. I was able to extend my enlistment and get out of combat, and I'm assigned to the intelligence office in My Tho. For various reasons that I can't go into, I volunteered for one more mission, and that action almost killed me. I have four months left on my tour of duty."

"You have been through a lot and are very lucky to be alive," Tuyen said. "I honor you for fighting for my country and respect you for your bravery. If not for people like you, Vietnam would be a Communist country, and I do not want that to happen."

Tuyen's statement brought tears of joy to my eyes.

"You must rest now, and I will return with other treats tomorrow."

After she left, I dreamed peacefully about the beautiful Vietnamese girl with long black hair who had brought solace to my soul. I had no idea that most of Tuyen's history was fictitious. She was pleased with herself for making contact with a member of the intelligence office in My Tho and thought only of how she could extract important information from me. She was totally committed to the Communist cause and the takeover of South Vietnam by the Communists.

During the first week of my healing process, I was almost pleased that I had been wounded, since the incident lead to a relationship with Tuyen. I looked forward to seeing her every day, longing for her company and her feigned innocence. I consciously wished that my wound would heal slowly so I would have more time to spend with Tuyen, who had quickly become the highlight of my day.

When we did have time together, I spoke at length about my life back home, leaving out only my relationship with Jeri. When I was able to get around in a wheel chair, I claimed to be weak and she volunteered to help me. Tuyen told me about her early life on the rubber plantation and how life had radically changed after her father was forced from the plantation by the Viet Cong. She spoke of how cruel the Viet Cong had been to her family, how proud she was of her brothers serving with the ARVN forces, and how much she worried about her mother. I was enthralled and sympathetic.

It became apparent to the other nurses and aids that Tuyen and I were becoming an item. This had happened before, as the wounded were particularly vulnerable to loving attention. No one paid particular attention, as all the nurses had sympathy for their patients and all the single Vietnamese females were looking to establish a relationship with an American. Some among them were spies who obviously approved of the relationship. The doctors were too busy to notice.

This routine continued for another week, until I became able to maneuver around the hospital on crutches. It was obvious that I would return to my desk job after over two weeks in the hospital. Because our relationship had become personal, Tuyen and I arranged to meet at an upscale restaurant. She appeared very reticent at first about this meeting due to the traditional conservatism of Vietnamese society but finally agreed to meet me two days later. I knew that appearing in public with her wouldn't be a problem, as many GI s had set up relationships with Vietnamese girls and publicly flaunted those relationships. I returned to my assigned unit.

With everyone aware of my exploits with SOG, I was accorded the awe and respect of my fellow soldiers and officers. I was no longer allowed to associate with any members of the SOG teams, although I saw my slain comrades everywhere I went. What I did not understand was why there was no mention of the award of a Purple Heart for me. When I questioned my captain about the situation, he closed the door and informed me that all records of my mission had been destroyed due to the team's entrance into Cambodia. I had participated in a nonexistent action, thus, there was no record of my wound and would be no Purple Heart. So much for valor.

I immersed myself in day-to-day activities awaiting my date with Tuyen. The rendezvous was the center of my attention. I cleaned up as best I could with the limited civilian wardrobe I had and appeared at the appointed restaurant a half-hour early, nervous as a teenager on his first date. I was surprised to see Tuyen arrive at the restaurant with a matronly, very refined Vietnamese lady as her escort. She explained that it was a Vietnamese custom for proper young ladies to be escorted on dates by older, more experienced relatives. Tuyen felt she must observe the custom out of respect for her mother and had enlisted the aid of the aunt of one of her roommates. All of the other American soldiers in the restaurant were with unaccompanied Vietnamese bar girls. Impressed by Tu yen's need to do the appropriate thing, I was more enamored than ever.

We had an enchanting evening with no alcohol consumed and every rule of etiquette observed. Tuyen and I agreed that we would see one another at the PX, and I returned to the barracks walking on air. She was closing her trap. In reality, of course, Tuyen's companion had been Comrade Long, her control agent in the Viet Cong infrastructure. Her purpose in accompanying Tuyen to her first formal date with me was to analyze my potential as an intelligence source and impress me with Tu yen's cultural values. Comrade Long spoke English quite well and was impressed by my position in the intelligence office, my supposed naivety, and my devotion to Tuyen. Comrade Long concluded that I would be a gold mine of information. She was unaware of Tuyen's commitment to Van but well aware of her involvement with Colonel Khan. She was very supportive of Tuyen, both because she wished to please Colonel Khan and because she saw a younger version of herself in Tuyen. Comrade Long would do absolutely anything to achieve the goals of the Communist cause.

Tuyen was at her normal checkout position at the PX the next couple of days and also continued to volunteer at the hospital. She saw me three days after our dinner and arranged to see me at the hospital later, as I had a legitimate excuse to be there for a checkup and visits with some of the more seriously wounded soldiers I'd met during my stay. We met quietly and arranged to have dinner several days hence at a villa supposedly occupied by Comrade Long. This much was true, but the villa also acted as a Viet Cong safe house. Unbeknownst to me, all conversations at the house were recorded, making it an ideal location for absorbing anything I might divulge of American operations.

I arrived at the appointed time with flowers. Tuyen greeted me in a beautiful white Ao Dai dress, and I was awestruck by her beauty. That time she was unaccompanied. We had a lovely time getting to know each other, and she prepared a sumptuous dinner. Ours was a very tentative exploration of each others emotional and mental state, as each of us had a lot to lose if our relationship was discovered. Our physical relationship was confined to hand holding and quick, platonic kisses. The evening was a huge success for both of us. I believed I had found a soul mate, while Tuyen knew she was planting the seeds for domination of my soul and the extraction of allied intelligence.

CHAPTER
13

Colonel Khan spent his time in Saigon planning and preparing for the coming TET offensive and the rebuilding of the Viet Cong supply and training facilities in Cambodia destroyed by the B-52 attacks carried out under Van's leadership, although in smaller, dispersed locations. Van had learned valuable lessons: never place all your eggs in one basket, and trust no one but yourself to attain your goals, especially not Colonel Khan or others in positions of command.

Colonel Khan was summoned to a high-level command meeting in Cambodia in early October of 1967. The entire higher command of the NVA and Viet Cong organizations were being called together in secrecy in tunnels deep in the Cambodian jungle. General Giap, the overall commander of the efforts to oust the allied forces from Vietnam, directed the conference. This had never happened before. If the allied forces were able to detect this meeting and capture or kill the attendees, the war would be over. Cut off the head and the body dies. But there were no leaks to the allies, and the conference went according to plan.

General Giap revealed that through January of 1968, the intense attacks would continue at Dak To and Khe San. The primary value of Dak To, a mountain town in the central highlands, was its proximity to the Ho Chi Minh trail. The NVA dug in at the top of the mountain and lured American forces to attack reinforced bunkers, thereby engaging more and more forces. Khe San, a Marine outpost on the DMZ, was highly vulnerable to artillery attacks from the surrounding mountains. Given the isolation of Khe San and the difficulty of resupply through the monsoon season, it was the perfect location for the Marines to tie up a great majority of their forces in an effort to prove the invincibility of American military power.

By defending Khe San, the American military command made it obvious that they hadn't learned anything from the French defeat at Dien Bien Phu in the early 1950s. During that battle, the French general brought in two divisions of troops into the valley of Dien Bien Phu, which was surrounded by mountains the French did not control. This was done because the French believed that the North Vietnamese didn't possess artillery pieces and thus were vulnerable.

The French were wrong. The North Vietnamese received artillery pieces from the Chinese and the North Koreans and drug them up the mountains by hand. When these huge pieces of equipment began to slip down the mountain in the mud, committed North Vietnamese soldiers threw themselves under the wheels to act as brakes. The North Vietnamese shelled the French for two months, and, when defeat was inevitable, the French general in charge committed suicide on the battlefield. The French surrendered, and ten thousand of their soldiers became prisoners of war, some used as bargaining chips and held captive for ten years. The ultimate irony of the situation was that these were not regular French Army troops but two divisions of French Foreign Legion.

1. The North Vietnamese destroyed two divisions of the French Foreign Legion, and the Americans thought they could do better fifteen years later. General Giaps overall plan was to pin down large numbers of Allied troops at Dak

76

To and Khe San during the latter part of 1967 and early 1968. In the meantime, Viet Cong and North Vietnamese Army activity would diminish in all other areas of Vietnam, lulling the allies into complacency and a belief that pacification of the countryside was working. Meanwhile, supplies and armaments flowed down the Ho Chi Minh trail and through Sihanoukville and the Cambodian ports, and Communist cadre continued to be recruited and trained.

The ultimate goal was to initiate a countrywide attack during the holy TET holidays, when a cease-fire would be in effect. The Communist command would use the element of surprise in hopes of a general uprising in the south that would defeat the American and ARVN forces. The Communist command was willing to roll the dice in a major offensive in the hopes of complete victory.

Colonel Kan realized that the tone of the directive indicated that there would be a general lessening of activity in the Mekong Delta and a great deal of emphasis on stockpiling of supplies and munitions and the recruiting and training of troops. He was confident that his decision not to eliminate Van as his commander in the Mekong Delta had been a wise move, as Van was clearly a great motivator and organizer. He was ruthless, and totally committed to the Communist cause.

The issue that most concerned Colonel Khan was keeping those plans from the allied forces for approximately four months. He also realized that the NVA command was willing to sacrifice the entire Viet Cong military force in the cause of victory, with the intent of ultimately replacing him and his men with NVA personnel. Colonel Khan devoted as much of his time to solidifying his connections within the NVA as he did planning for the coming assault—and he continued to stockpile his skimmed funds in Swiss banks. No matter which side was victorious, Colonel Khan's ultimate plan was to escape Vietnam a rich man, abandoning his wife and family for some exotic locale with Tuyen. There really was no difference between Colonel Khan and the corrupt ARVN officer corps.

After the high-echelon meetings in Cambodia, Colonel Khan met with Van, who was ecstatic to hear of the coming planned TET offensive and realized that he would play a pivotal role. Van had no problem recruiting more Mekong Delta villagers to the cause. If the native populace had not been alienated by the Allied forces through the killing of family and friends and the destruction of their villages, Van could always resort to physical and emotional threats. His primary goals were ensuring that existing Communist forces retreated from confrontation with Allied forces and keeping new recruits at a high professionalism without exposing them to combat. His major problem revolved around attaining these objectives while revealing as little as possible about the coming offensive.

Van could also see that with such a massive attack planned, the Viet Cong forces would suffer immense casualties, leaving the organization vulnerable to takeover by the NVA. He continued to make every effort to not only ensure that he had the admiration and respect of the Viet Cong command but also that the NVA hierarchy knew of his accomplishments and capabilities. He was determined to survive the coming offensive as a dedicated Communist and dreamt of eventually reuniting with his Communist lover, Tuyen.

CHAPTER
14

I stuck with my daily routine and constantly daydreamed about Tuyen. SOG activities continued at a high level, but all the information I received came through the usual channels. By the end of October, it had become apparent that there had been a lessening of enemy mainline activity and a return to the old small-scale attacks, an increase in sniper activity, and an increasing number of casualties from booby traps. The Allied High Command attributed these successes to severing the supply routes along the Ho Chi Minh trail and eliminating vast numbers of the Viet Cong cadre through the pacification program.

I knew that a quick solution to the war would be the bombing of the ports of Haiphong and Sihanoukville, which would result in an 80 percent reduction in supplies available to the Communists. Diplomatic policies had prevented this. The Allied command had no clue as to the coming TET offensive. Van instructed his cadre to refrain from direct contact with the enemy, trying instead to keep his experienced troops actively harassing the enemy and gradually inserting more and more Communist troops into the major cities of the Mekong Delta and Saigon. The Communists gradually moved munitions from Cambodia into supply depots throughout the area as the Allied forces became increasingly secure in the idea that they were winning the conflict through pacification.

Our pacification program consisted of establishing Allied military outposts of ten to twenty men throughout South Vietnam to give the local inhabitants a sense of security and at the same time provide agricultural advisors and modern equipment to the rural farmers. This pacification of the countryside worked in some areas where the Communists were weak, but in more areas than not, the very troops who were to provide the peasants with security were Viet Cong. As a result, the program was doing the recruiting for the enemy.

Colonel Khan spent all his time in Saigon perfecting the attack plan that would be applied to his area of operations, which extended from the Plain of Reeds in the south to Saigon itself. This was a unique area 90 percent of which was comprised of rice paddies fed by the monsoon rains of the tropics and the fertile silt of the Mekong. The Delta held 50 percent of the population of South Vietnam, and it had been said that if the Delta could be properly cultivated by controlling the flow of water, all of China could be fed.

Because of the concentration of the population, this area was ideal for recruitment by the Viet Cong. The average farmer tilled his fields from dawn to dusk, producing a poverty level existence at best. Due to the ongoing conflict, the Mekong Delta farmer was paying a high tax to the South Vietnamese government and paying duty to the Viet Cong at the same time. The peasant farmer's only concern was for the survival of his family and being left alone to till his fields in peace. His fondest wish was for the war to end.

ecruiters reported a tremendous increase in new recruits as the war progressed, largely due to increased nationalism, a dislike of Western morality, and continuing success on the battlefield by NVA and Viet Cong forces. The more recruits that came in, the more cadre needed to train them, and this entailed not only field training but also brainwashing in the Communist mentality. The biggest hurdle to a recruiter was convincing the recruits that it was necessary to annihilate all who stood in the path of Communist victory and that that often entailed eliminating friends, neighbors, and even family. The new recruits had to believe that the cause demanded that they use any atrocity, any terror tactic against any opposition to achieve the goals of Communism.

The Vietnamese people's intrinsic need to be independent of the control of any foreign power played right into the hands of the Communists. They had been controlled by foreign powers for many centuries. The Chinese, the French, the Japanese, and now the Americans had all taken turns ruling the country of Vietnam and its people. The French had referred to Vietnam as the Pearl of the Orient and had used it as a vacation area for their upper class and for its abundant supply of rubber.

The Vietnamese populace had been enslaved by foreign powers for centuries, and the truth was that the average Vietnamese would rather be enslaved by another Vietnamese than a foreign power. Communist philosophy offered a bright new world to the common man. Colonel Khan used all these sentiments to his advantage and was regarded by his NVA controllers as a prime mover in recruiting the average Vietnamese farmer to the revolutionary cause.

Naturally, every civilian casualty caused by Allied actions motivated ten relatives to join the Communist cause, and this type of recruiting multiplied daily. Colonel Khans biggest problem had now become logistics. In order to coordinate massive attacks against the Allied forces during the coming TET offensive, munitions had to be stockpiled everywhere within Colonel Khan's area of operations. Obviously the soldiers who comprised the main fighting force in Cambodia could not be moved en masse into all areas of the Mekong Delta and Saigon at one time, as this would result in the decimation of the Viet Cong as a fighting force. Troops had to be slowly inserted into the fabric of South Vietnamese daily life so as not to attract attention, and they had to stockpile munitions without being detected. It would only take a minor leak to jeopardize the coming offensive.

Colonel Khan therefore decided that each Viet Cong unit would be under the impression that their attack would be an isolated instance and would have no knowledge of the breadth and scope of the action. He instituted a campaign of terror among the local populace, and the Communists sacrificed many innocent lives in order to achieve their goals. Colonel Khan devoted a large amount of his time to organizing the movement of supplies and munitions into strategic staging areas in the Mekong Delta and the outskirts of Saigon. These areas held numerous inconspicuous hiding places and tens of thousands of Communist sympathizers, from coolie drivers to bar girls.

The plan was to hide weapons and ammunition among the general populace, each individual responsible for the care of the same, and with no one aware of the general attack or its timing. The security forces surrounding Saigon and all the major cities of the Delta, both American and South Vietnamese, were too busy guarding against terrorist attacks and immersed in satisfying their carnal desires to pay attention to the day-to-day activities of the general public.

The most serious problem was the transportation of vast amounts of munitions and supplies out of Cambodia under cover of darkness and the spreading of these items among the standard transportation units of the Mekong Delta. They used trucks, sampans, coolies, water buffalo, and virtually anything that moved in the normal course of daily transportation, and no one vehicle transported items in quantity. The security forces of the Allies concentrated most of their forces on monitoring nighttime movements, and if any entity was detected, the size of the supplies and munitions carried were so minimal that no suspicion of a large-scale movement was aroused. Detection could always lead to the discovery of the overall plan, but since none of these individuals knew the entire scope of the operation, revelation was impossible. The plan was brilliant in its simplicity, and the operation was never ending.

The movement of trained troops into the major cities of the Mekong Delta and Saigon was another problem. Colonel Khan decided that this movement would be delayed until early January, with the exception for senior cadre members, who were in place by early December. In the meantime, the recruiting and training of rank and file troops continued at a furious pace. The troops were not aware that they were cannon fodder.

Once these issues were addressed, Colonel Khan concentrated his efforts on maintaining communications with his field commanders in the Mekong Delta while at the same time coordinating other attack plans with Viet Cong commanders in the South and keeping clear lines of communication with his superiors in the North Vietnamese hierarchy. This allowed him to solidify his command position within the Communist party while increasing the immense buildup of supplies and munitions in his area of operations.

Colonel Khan continued to collect bribes and send money to his Swiss bank accounts. He had no time to visit Tuyen but was kept informed of her relationship with me and was pleased by it—anything to aid the cause. Colonel Khan developed a plan for the future that would allow him to escape Vietnam at the proper time no matter who won the war, and Tuyen would accompany him. She wasn't aware of his plan, but if she refused, she would be eliminated. Colonel Khan intended to abandon Tuyen if necessary and live a life of luxury in some agreeable country. The Communist cause was only a means to an end for him.

Feverish activity consumed Van's days and nights. He had a major issue with the continual stream of supplies and munitions arriving in Cambodia down the Ho Chi Minh trail. He couldn't afford another fiasco such as the SOG attack. His cadre found large caves deep in the Cambodian jungle and never left supplies where they could be seen from the air. At the same time, munitions and supplies were constantly being shipped into the Mekong Delta and Saigon. Since the majority of the offensive activity had diminished in these areas and was restricted to harassing activities, casualties had been greatly diminished, thereby releasing experienced cadre for the training of raw recruits in Cambodia.

Van was working twenty-hour days fueled by the adrenalin rush of plans for the coming attack. He had no contact with T She was left to her own devices, maneuvering through the politics of Colonel Khan's advances and trying to get intelligence from me. Van was in daily contact with Colonel Khan and had noticed a decidedly frigid relationship develop since the debacle of the SOG attack. Whereas before, Van was almost a son to Colonel Khan, now, the relationship was all business. Van preferred it that way.

Van also became aware of Colonel Khan's theft of millions from the revolution, and his attitude changed from admiration to loathing. Van now knew that Colonel Khan was only interested in enriching himself; the Communist cause meant nothing to him. He realized that Colonel Khan was a necessary evil in the command structure of the revolution, but Van was determined to eliminate Colonel Khan after the offensive, or at the very least inform the Colonel's superiors of his actions. He was also aware of the relationship between Tuyen and Colonel Khan and had complete trust in her. She must do what she must do in order to maintain her position in the Communist hierarchy.

As soon as possible, Van made arrangements to rendezvous with Tuyen and warn her of the dangers intrinsic to her relationship with Colonel Khan. They met at the beginning of December, and Van revealed everything he knew about Colonel Khan's plans to her. She told him that recently, Colonel Khan had mentioned living outside the country after the victory over the Allied forces, but she had not felt this plan would include her. Van was most insistent that she be ready at all times to flee to his protection upon any indication that Colonel Khan was becoming a threat, or if Tuyen's relationship with me might jeopardize her position.

The most dangerous thing that could happen would be if Van and Tu yen's relationship became apparent to Colonel Khan. Van was sure that the Colonel would personally kill both of them. Van and Tuyen renewed their emotional commitment to each other and the cause and made contingency plans in case she had to flee. Van made it clear that Tuyen had to play dual roles of being devoted to Colonel Khan and being devoted to me while ultimately pledging her devotion to Van. At all costs, she must not allow Comrade Long to become aware of her relationship with Van. If somehow became aware of their relationship, it would be a death sentence.

CHAPTER

15

I was pleased with my relationship with Tuyen. My reality was anchored in the moment, infused by the beauty and simplicity of the relationship. After being reduced to an emotional zombie by the military, my emotional soul had been reawakened by our relationship. My every waking moment revolved around my next meeting with her. Although I saw her often at the hospital, this didn't allow for any real social contact. All I could do was moon over her with puppy dog eyes, waiting to be petted. She was quite adept at manipulating my need for her, both physically and emotionally, even though she had no experience in these matters.

Finally, in early November, Tuyen agreed to dinner alone at Comrade Long's villa. This encounter began much differently than any other and very differently than I'd expected. She spent a great deal of time teaching me Vietnamese words, and the time passed swiftly. Finally I was overcome by my emotions and caressed her entire body. She responded as any sensual woman would, and her soft moans of delight reverberated throughout the villa. Our lips met in sensual ecstasy as we slowly removed our clothes. I had never experienced anything like it in my entire life—physically or emotionally.

Tuyen performed as only a sensual woman could, methodically bringing me to the heights of Nirvana. Emotionally, she only wished the experience was with Van rather than me but performed as required in order to net her catch. We convulsed in a paroxysm of sexual release and bliss. I *was* overcome by the grandeur of my first sexual and emotional commitment. Tuyen was pleased by what she had accomplished and pleasantly surprised, as this was the first time she had enjoyed the physical act of sex. She realized that this encounter with me was far superior to any physical encounter she'd had with Colonel Khan. I stayed until dawn and professed my everlasting love for her and she for me. My declarations were heartfelt, but Tuyen had an agenda.

We promised to see each other at the hospital as much as possible and meet at her "Aunt's" villa at least once a week. I snuck into the barracks, had a quick shower, and reported for my normal routine. I walked around in a daze. Tuyen reported on the evening's events to Comrade Long. All parties were well pleased, albeit for different reasons. Tuyen realized that I was vulnerable to revealing intelligence information of importance. She arranged with Comrade Long to have access to the villa for a three-day weekend, during which she could use her sexual wiles to extract intelligence information from me.

We met on a Friday afternoon in mid-November, and Tuyen was well aware that Comrade Long and Colonel Khan were pushing for important information from me. She was prepared to interrogate me with an assortment of intoxicants ranging from alcohol to low-level hallucinogens. We began with an array of Asian foods as she explained that she wanted me to experience all the exotic flavors of her homeland.

She prepared our sumptuous meal while fending off my amorous advances, declaring that we must proceed slowly and have plenty of time to reach Nirvana. She had already scented the air with various sensual aromas meant to relax and invigorate our senses. After a delicious meal, we retired to the garden area with its relaxing waterfall and beautiful koi ponds. We engaged in slow, amorous lovemaking wherein I released all my military rigidity and relaxed, shedding any mental defenses I had.

After a long period of lovemaking, we succumbed to the delights of mind-expanding drugs. She slowly but surely attained her goal of getting me to talk about my work in the intelligence office. I began by telling her how foreign I found the regimental discipline imposed by the military on all its members and sharing my eventual realization that, with the large number of soldiers necessary for accomplishing the military's mission, it was an absolute must that this discipline be a fact of day-to-day life. I informed her that when I was exposed to combat, I hated it, but I realized that the strict regimen imposed was an absolute necessity and contributed to our chances of survival in combat.

I felt that my relationship with Tuyen had reconnected my emotional spinal chord and allowed me to feel again. When I told her that, she knew that I was ready to be interrogated. She innocently inquired about my feelings for my current duties. I started slowly, telling her about my boring day-to-day activities, but as I continued to speak, the relaxation of the hallucinogens took hold and I told her how the intelligence office in My Tho operated.

I went on at great length about how the Allied forces had informers in virtually every hamlet in the Delta and thus felt that they had a good feel for the future activities of the Viet Cong. I also told Tuyen that, with our network of spies, our intelligence community felt they were on top of enemy activities. I went on to say that the lessening of enemy activity over the last several months had been a result of the destruction of many enemy supply depots and heavy bombing of the Ho Chi Minh trail.

"I and my superiors feel that the pacification program in the countryside is becoming increasingly successful," I explained. "As a result, fewer and fewer of the populace are being recruited by the Viet Cong."

Tuyen said little, letting me feel comfortable in my stream of consciousness. We fell into a drug-induced sleep, floating to Nirvana in our cloud of hallucinogens.

Tuyen knew that she had been successful in her first interrogation of me, but she also knew that there was much more valuable information to be obtained. She was surprised to discover how easy it had been. She had underestimated her abilities as a temptress. She hoped that she would learn a great deal more in the next few days.

We began the second day with more lovemaking. She fulfilled every sexual fantasy I had ever had. She had approached the three-day rendezvous as a mission she had to fulfill in order to extract intelligence, but she found that she had been able to raise the level of her sexual gratification to heights not experienced previously. She still held firmly to her mission but at the same time was enjoyed the romance immensely.

She prepared a lavish Vietnamese breakfast, and we decided to take a tour of her My Tho. We toured the fish market, the old French fort, the bazaars, and finally the memorial to all those who had died in previous conflicts. Unknowingly, she was expressing her strongly held beliefs in Vietnamese independence and her sorrow about the suffering her people had endured at the hands of the invaders. I was certainly sympathetic to the sufferings of her people but also believed in my heart that my government's efforts to stabilize the South Vietnamese regime and institute Democracy into Indo-China, was a worthwhile effort. Neither of us expressed these views to the other while drinking in the beauty of the city of My Tho, we focused on our feelings for each other.

Upon returning to the villa, Tuyen gave me a deeply sexual massage. The addition of hallucinogenic drugs had me speaking of my experiences with the Riverine unit and the losses we had experienced on Toy Son island. Tuyen didn't let on that she was raised on the island. She realized that Van was the sniper who had inflicted many of the casualties on my unit and felt sad that the man she was now with was the target of her one true love. I also spoke of the destruction of A Company on June 19 and how that event had convinced me to extend my term of service in order to remove myself from combat.

Tuyen realized that the destruction of A Company had led me to her, and ironically, Van had organized and spearheaded that event. She felt sad for all involved that this horrible revolution had led us down this path of destruction, and she abhorred the idea that one of us might someday cause another's death. She wept in my arms. I thought that maybe she was sympathizing with what I had been through, but her heart was being torn in half by two patriotic men. I caressed and consoled her, which lead to a repeat of the immense sexual satisfaction and emotional pleasure we derived from each other.

I lay exhausted in her arms. Without any coaxing, I told her about my choosing to be assigned to the intelligence office at My Tho, rather than be assigned to a humdrum desk job in Saigon. I detailed how I found these intelligence duties rewarding, especially when my security clearance was raised. I spoke of my distaste for the bar scene and the drunken ways of my fellow soldiers, my physical regimen, and my day-to-day contact with SOG team members. I told her that I relished hearing about their experiences in Cambodia and Laos and about my need for the adrenaline-pumping experiences they spoke of. I told her that the SOG teams were severely understaffed and that I had volunteered to go on one of their missions in order to experience the thrill of combat and because I had to prove to myself that I wasn't a coward. Finally, I talked about my experience on the mission into Cambodia and how our team had penetrated the Viet Cong defenses and called in air strikes on the camp there.

That last revelation in particular constituted a major breach of security, but I wanted to share my life with Tuyen. When I told her I was the only survivor of the team, she cried, not only for my pain but because she knew that Van's men had tried to annihilate my team and vice versa.

We sank into an exhausted sleep, each dreaming about the future in very different ways. We spent our final day together in each other's arms. Physically and emotionally exhausted, we parted lovingly into the early evening hours. Neither of our lives would ever be the same.

CHAPTER
16

Tuyen was immediately interrogated by Comrade Long. She detailed how I had revealed to her that the Allied forces felt that the lessening of combat incidents in the Mekong Delta was a direct result of the village pacification program and that the diminishing available supplies being transported down the Ho Chi Minh trail was due to heavy Allied bombing. She explained that the Allies had no inkling of the planned TET offensive and no knowledge of the infiltration of troops and munitions into Saigon and the major cities throughout Vietnam.

This information was critical to the Viet Cong and North Vietnamese High Command, as it reinforced their current activities and made them bolder in their approach. Comrade Long complimented Tuyen on what she had learned and passed the information on to Colonel Khan. Tuyen was ordered to continue her affair with me and gain more information.

Tuyen sent the report to Van unbeknownst to Colonel Khan, emphasizing the activities of the Riverine unit on VC island, my presence during the annihilation of A Company, and my activities with the SOG unit that destroyed Van's main base camp in Cambodia. Van was gratified to receive this information and amazed at how mine and his own life had become intertwined. Van didn't approve of Tu yen's involvement with me but realized its importance to the war effort. He vowed to eventually have me eliminated.

For now, his total focus was on preparing for the coming offensive. Armaments were critical, and Van was pleased by the continuing stream of supplies coming down the Ho Chi Minh trail in spite of continued Allied bombing. The superhuman efforts of these coolies, whether driving a truck or acting as pack animals, were phenomenal. Continually harassed by B-52 air strikes, these people had to contend with monsoons, jungle terrain, disease, lack of food, SOG teams, and physical degradation.

These human cargo bearers had already died psychologically, committing themselves to the cause of revolution and embracing the sacrifice of their lives. Van realized that these people would make ideal suicide bombers. From each group, Van culled what appeared to be the most dedicated members and formed them into sapper teams, training them in sabotage and infiltration. By the end of November 1967, he had three hundred of these sapper teams organized and trained from the Ho Chi Minh cadre.

Van trained them personally, and his greatest aim was to show them how to assimilate into the social fabric of Mekong Delta society. These were all North Vietnamese and therefore spoke in a different accent than the South Vietnamese and had different social mannerisms. It would be like an Irishman with thick brogue trying to pass himself off as a native of Alabama. They had to eliminate certain phrases and mannerisms from their day-to-day lives and refine their accents so that the South Vietnamese way of speaking became second nature.

Van spent indoctrinating the cadre. They would have to blend in with the local populace for thirty days prior to the TET offensive. They were separated into teams of three to five, followed by a great deal of mixing and reintegrating of teams as the most cohesive pairings emerged. By the end of December 1967, they were ready to die for the cause. Colonel Khan had entered into the most critical and demanding phase of planning for the TET offensive. He had to spend a great deal of time interfacing with the North Vietnamese Command, meticulously detailing and fine tuning the offensive.

It had been very difficult to get the Command to understand how the war in the Mekong Delta differed greatly from what was going on in the central highlands. Central highlands activity had been increasingly based on conventional war tactics. The North Vietnamese fortified the top of a commanding mountain and drew the Americans into an assault. The battle went on for weeks. Eventually the Allied forces gained the crest of the mountain, only to discover that the North Vietnamese had disappeared. The Allied forces would then retreat and the North Vietnamese would reoccupy the abandoned mountaintop. It was a very costly way to wage war and very demoralizing to the Allied forces when they were forced to retake the same objective over and over.

In the Mekong Delta, war was solely based on small-unit attacks, booby traps, and snipers. Every now and then, there was a major battle, as when the Viet Cong wiped out A Company. But this action was only triggered when the Viet Cong had an overwhelming edge.

First, Colonel Khan had to convince the North Vietnamese that this type of warfare had to continue in the Mekong Delta, keeping the Allies confused as to what was really being planned. Colonel Khan's challenge was to indoctrinate his squad, platoon, and company commanders in the tactics of massive frontal assault of the type planned and somehow arrange it so that these individual units would be able to act as one unit when the offensive ensued. Colonel Khan eventually convinced the North Vietnamese that the continual harassment of Allied troops in the Mekong Delta was extremely vital at a diminished level and that he needed time to coordinate the training of his cadre in the art of conventional warfare. He received the OK to proceed at the beginning of November 1967.

To accomplish his objectives, Colonel Khan had to depend heavily on Van, whom he instructed to appoint five hundred cadre leaders in control of two thousand platoon leaders, who would in turn appoint ten thousand squad leaders, each in charge of five-man units. Twenty-five thousand troops were committed to the Saigon region, ten thousand to the My Tho area, and ten thousand to the Can Tho region. The platoon leaders were all experienced combat troops with a great desire to sacrifice their lives for their country but limited seniority and experience. The squad leaders were relatively new to combat but highly dedicated, and members of the five-man teams were, as usual, the youngest and least experienced but most enthusiastic of the fighting force. In other words: cannon fodder.

Van made it clear to the cadre leaders that secrecy was of the utmost importance and anyone suspected of revealing specifics of the attack would be eliminated immediately, as would their families. Only the cadre leaders knew specifics of the overall plan, with the remaining members of the attack force aware only of the activities in their assigned area. After making these selections, Van had to devise a simple communications system starting from the top down. All communication from Van's command post to his cadre leaders was based on encrypted radio messages. The same was true of communications from the cadre to the platoon leaders and so on.

It had been decided that the attack would begin throughout South Vietnam at 0200 on January 31, 1968. The attack would be coordinated throughout South Vietnam in order to cause as much confusion as possible and optimize victory. The Communist mentality was such that they were convinced the general Vietnamese population would rise up against the Allied forces and support the revolution.

Hu'ng had served Van faithfully for two years, ever since Van left Toy Son island. Hu'ng was raised in the town of Can Tho and now had a wife and two children. He was Van's right-hand man when they'd wiped out A Company. He was also present when the SOG team discovered Van's supply and training location and called in the B-52s. Hu'ng was well aware of Van's rage and need for revenge.

He was also a spy for Colonel Khan, reporting Van's every move to him. Colonel Khan trusted no one. Over the course of time,

Hu'ng had become convinced that he was more capable than Van, and Colonel Khan encouraged this idea. When Hu'ng became aware of the master plan for the TET offensive, it was apparent to him that if Van performed well, his star would continue to ascend—and Hu'ng would never become the leader he knew he was capable of being. He was an egotistical man with great aspirations, and the thought ate at his very soul. Hu'ng was privy to all the plans for the coming offensive, as he was one of the leaders of the five hundred cadre leaders. He was an amoral man, similar to Colonel Khan. But Hu'ng differed from Colonel Khan in that he worshipped his family, and everything he had done had been to improve their position and happiness.

As the attack plan for the TET offensive became apparent, Hu'ng believed there was no chance of a Communist victory. The Allied firepower was too great, and their air superiority would annihilate any conventional warfare tactics. Hu'ng could not see how this attack could be coordinated over the entire country without the Allied command becoming aware of it. He decided to betray the cause in order to survive and have any kind of future for himself and his family. His betrayal obviously would include Colonel Khan and Van, but this didn't disturb him in the least. He was a man who lived by the code of the jungle: survival of the fittest. He just needed to devise a plan to contact the Allies without raising suspicion.

In his capacity as corps commander, Hu'ng had been assigned to the My Tho district, as Van did not want to have any commander associate with the people of his own residence. Van did this so that the commanders would have an unemotional view of the people they were recruiting and training and would eventually have to send to their deaths. As a result, Hu'ng spent a great deal of time in My Tho. He surveyed the American compound, ascertained who the intelligence personnel were, and made a deal that would protect both himself and his family.

He could travel freely around My Tho in his role as a trader of agricultural commodities and decided to attempt to contact an enlisted soldier, who would be much more approachable than an officer. For several weeks he observed the comings and goings of the enlisted personnel assigned to the intelligence office at My Tho and noticed one individual who seemed to mingle across all ranks with ease. This was critical to Hu'ng because it would not do him any good to contact anyone who did not have access to those in authority.

He approached me while I was buying some fresh vegetables at the open-air market. Hu'ng engaged me in casual conversation and impressed me with his knowledge of the city of My Tho. I was intrigued by him, as I wished to learn more about the city in order to impress Tuyen. Hu'ng and I arranged to have lunch the next day. I thought about him all day and into the evening. I had told no one about Hu'ng because, so far, there was nothing to tell. I reminded myself to be wary at lunch for any signs that he was anything but what he said he was.

We had a leisurely lunch, and Hu'ng shared his wide range of knowledge about My Tho. As we settled back with a drink after lunch, Hu'ng decided that he could trust me. When he revealed his true role as a prominent member of the Viet Cong, I almost bolted from the restaurant but soon realized that he posed no immediate threat to me. Hu'ng revealed that he was present during the annihilation of A Company and when the B-52s destroyed the training camp in Cambodia. I didn't reveal my presence at these two incidents, waiting to see where his soliloquy was going.

Hu'ng professed his disillusionment with the Communist propaganda and his desire to go over to the side of the allies. He hinted that there was a huge offensive being planned throughout Vietnam, that he was privy to the information, and that he would reveal all to the Allies once he had assurances of safe haven for himself and his family. We parted company planning to meet again on Monday. He impressed upon me the need for secrecy and that time was of the essence.

Friday evening, I met with Tuyen at the villa. She had a sumptuous Vietnamese meal prepared, and various sensual scents filled the air. Gradually, she relaxed me after a tumultuous week. After consuming copious amounts of food, I lay in her arms and spoke of the future. I expressed my love for her and my desire to bring her back to the states. She immediately questioned how this could be accomplished. I told her I had been looking into the possible procedures, and, although the process was lengthy, it was possible.

Tuyen expressed concern for her family on Toy Son island, and I assured her I had considered this situation and that I would be allowed to sponsor them also. She replied that she would need time to think about things. Of course, she knew in her heart of hearts that none of this was possible due to her commitment to Van and the Communist cause. Tuyen also knew that any investigation of her background would be disastrous, as everything she'd told me about herself had been a lie. We agreed not to discuss the matter further until she'd had time to think about things and slipped into the passionate realm of lovemaking.

We spent Saturday exploring the markets of My Tho and, after a long lunch, we experimented with various hallucinogenic drugs. Ultimately, I was reduced to a sensual slave willing to reveal anything to Tuyen . I eventually spoke about my meeting with Hu'ng and my doubts about his veracity. She was immediately alert and coyly waited for me to reveal all the details, as she knew I would. I told her that Hu'ng knew of a plan for a large-scale Communist attack due to happen during TET. I also told her where Hu'ng and I were to meet for lunch on Monday.

Tuyen immediately found an excuse to go to the market for fresh vegetables. In reality, she went to make contact with local agents to pass on the information to Van. She didn't inform Comrade Long. She wanted this information available to Van only, so he could take all the credit for finding a traitor in his midst.

Tuyen returned to the Villa as I was awakening from a much-needed nap. She began preparing dinner, and I began again on the subject of marriage and her returning with me to the United States. She adamantly refused to discuss the matter further until had more time to think things through. The remainder of the evening was wrought with tension, and we retired early.

In the morning we had a quiet breakfast and separated lovingly with each of us having a lot to think about. She immediately contacted her Viet Cong links to Van told her that it would be necessary for her to be in the area where I was to meet Hu'ng Monday so that the Viet Cong agents could identify who he was and deal with him appropriately.

I met with Hu'ng as planned and pressed him for more details on future enemy activity. He indicated that there was a tremendous buildup of arms and supplies going on all over South Vietnam and that the activity in the Central Highlands and Khe Sahn was a diversionary tactic. He would say no more until he and his family were brought into the Allied camp and given protection. I agreed to pass on the information to my superiors and meet with him again on Friday. Hu'ng again impressed upon me that time was of the essence.

Viet Cong agents watched us, aided by Tuyen, who success-fully identified Hu'ng. I returned to my office, requested a meet-ing with one of the senior intelligence officers, and detailed my meetings with Hu'ng. After conferring with several officers, they came to the conclusion that he was a lower-ranking Viet Cong operative who had made up the story to gain the confidence of the intelligence community, thereby gaining privileges for himself and his family. The outlook of these men was that the pacification program was a success and that no major offensive by the enemy was possible. Still, I was encouraged to keep in contact with Hu'ng to see where it led.

The evening of Hu'ng's meeting with me, he and his family were abducted by Viet Cong agents and transported to Van's head-quarters in the Cambodian jungle. Van took charge of his inter-rogation, asking him who the American soldier was that he'd had lunch with. Hu'ng replied that I was an American who worked as a clerk in the intelligence office and that he was trying to develop me as a source of information.

Van did not hesitate to use a cattle prod on Hu'ng to get him to tell the truth. When he refused to admit to anything more, Van tortured Hu'ng's wife in front of the children—beginning with a cattle prod and progressing to the bullwhip. When he still didn't talk, Van had five Viet Cong rape Hu'ng's wife repeatedly in front of her children. Her screams of agony filled the jungle. Still, he stuck to his story. Van then began to work on the children, breaking their fingers one by one.

Hu'ng could finally take no more and confessed to intent to betray the cause in order to protect himself and his family. He told Van that the American had expressed disbelief in the little that he had told him and required more proof.

Van then proceeded to break every bone in Hu'ng's body in a slow, methodical manner before finally torching the entire family. He did this in front of as many cadre as possible, and the message was clear: never betray Van or the Communist cause, as the consequences would be worse than death.

I waited patiently for Hu'ng to meet me at the appointed rendezvous. Not being a company man as the intelligence officers were, I was an outsider looking in. From this position, my mind was open to any possibility but needed further proof. I waited for several hours, but Hu'ng did not appear. My only knowledge of his whereabouts was based on information Hu'ng had told me about his activities as a trader of agriculture commodities. When I reported to my superiors that Hu'ng had failed to appear at the assigned meeting place, they were very smug in their "I told you so" attitude. I knew that there was no point in pursuing the whereabouts of Hu'ng, but I was determined to investigate the supposed coming offensive further on my own.

I haunted the agricultural markets in My Tho, making inquiries of everyone about Hu'ng. Everyone knew him, but no one had seen him recently. Not only did it appear that he had disappeared, it also occurred to me that he may have been a ruse all along. None of this made sense to me, since any communication from Hu'ng had been initiated by him. Given this fact, I remained convinced that he had legitimate information concerning a coming large-scale attack.

It seemed as though Hu'ng had disappeared. I was now on a one-man mission to find out if in fact there was such a plan, and if so, when it was to be implemented. I checked the Allied casualty rates daily and realized that over the last six months, there had been a steady decline in Allied casualties throughout South Vietnam—with the exception of the Dak To and Khe Sahn areas. Allied casualties had seen a 40 percent decline over the last six months, and no major battles had occurred from the Central Highlands to the Mekong Delta. At the same time, the pacification program in the rural areas of South Vietnam appeared to be having more and more success. It was as if the Viet Cong were playing football and saving their offense for the last half of the fourth quarter. I also checked the intelligence reports of activity along the Ho Chi Minh trail and found that the flow of supplies and munitions had increased substantially over the last six months.

I spoke with the SOG teams coming back from Cambodia and learned that it was becoming increasingly difficult to locate Viet Cong sanctuaries and supply depots. I tried to contact sources who were known to supply information about enemy activity, only to discover that everyone had turned deaf and dumb. It was all very suspicious. I compiled a report tracing my suspicions of a major enemy attack back to Hu'ng's allegations, the lessening of allied casualties, the increase in activity along the Ho Chi Minh trail, and the drying up of local information sources.

I learned from inside sources and news reports that the Johnson administration continually estimated enemy forces in Vietnam, North Vietnamese and Viet Cong combined, to be in the range of two hundred fifty thousand to three hundred thousand, whereas the consensus in Saigon through CIA analysis of enemy activity and information captured from enemy soldiers placed the numbers at between five and six hundred thousand.

The Johnson administration contended that enemy numbers were dwindling due to punishing losses in the field and resistance to enemy recruitment. The consensus in Saigon was that enemy numbers were on the rise due to infiltration and the commitment of the younger generation to reclaiming their country. All of this information convinced me that there were movements going on throughout South Vietnam in late 1967 that pointed to disaster for the Allied cause. Most importantly, a massive cover-up originating in the Johnson administration told the American public that enemy forces were far below CIA estimates. Furthermore, the general populace of South Vietnam was in favor of the removal of Allied forces and wanted to be in control of their own destiny.

But most importantly, a huge buildup of personnel and supplies during late 1967 pointed to some type of major offensive in early 1968. I proceeded to report my findings to members of the intelligence community I trusted and was told to concentrate on my clerical job and leave intelligence work to the professionals. In essence, I was told that my conclusions were so bizarre and based on such flimsy evidence that they could only assume that I had spent my evenings with my head in a whiskey bottle.

My only solace was dreams of Tuyen. We met again at the villa, where she had arranged for a cook and a maid to wait on us hand and foot over the weekend and for a masseuse to massage us to set the mood; we would not have to leave the villa. Of course, all were members of the Viet Cong intelligence community under the control of Van, and all conversations were being recorded in order to analyze any information she might miss.

Tuyen could tell immediately that I was preoccupied, and during our meal, I couldn't remove myself from what was bothering me. I drank quite a bit more than I was accustomed to. In the throes of my melancholy, I told Tuyen I believed that the Johnson administration was conducting a massive propaganda campaign intended to convince the American people that the allied forces were winning in Vietnam through doctored reports of Allied victories and underestimations of the enemy's strength and capabilities. I told her about the disappearance of Hu'ng and my inability to find any trace of his existence.

I told her that I continued to believe that enemy forces in South Vietnam were staging attacks at Dak To and Khe San as diversionary tactics while the Communist forces were building up manpower and supplies in South Vietnam in order to stage a major offensive sometime in the next few months. I explained that I was convinced that the lessening of enemy activity in the south over the last few months was a cover-up by the Communists in order to lull the Allies into complacency. I finally broke down in tears over my complete failure to convince the officers in the intelligence division of these facts and finally fell into a fitful sleep in Tuyen's arms.

The next day, we made no mention of the previous night's conversation. We instead spent a love-filled morning in each others arms, soaking up the peacefulness of our hideaway and confirming our commitment to each other. We parted late that afternoon, planning to meet the following weekend at our favorite restaurant.

CHAPTER
17

Immediately after my rendezvous with Tuyen , Comrade Long began passing on news of my suspicions about the coming offensive to Colonel Khan. He immediately realized that if I continued with my allegations of troop buildup and the possibility of a coming attack, someone higher up in the intelligence community would pay attention and the Communist's plans would be exposed.

He sent word of the situation to Van and instructed him to eliminate me at the first opportunity. Comrade Long was aware of the dinner date that Saturday between Tuyen and me at our favorite restaurant. She was also aware that I always arrived about a half-hour early to our meetings out of anticipation, so a plan was developed to send a terrorist squad to eliminate me with a bomb to make it look as though my death was the result of a random terrorist attack. By coordinating the attack for before Tuyen's arrival, she would be protected and the mission would be accomplished.

The plan was put into effect by Van, who was more than pleased to be the force behind my demise for several reasons. Obviously he was aware of the means by which Tuyen had extracted information from me, and although he believed that the end justified the means, he was still incensed by the relationship. He also realized that I had been on Toy Son island, had been present when A Company was annihilated, and was part of the SOG team that had instigated the attack on his supply and training camp in Cambodia. All these facts gave Van plenty of reason to desire my elimination.

The one thing he did not realize was the extent to which Tuyen had become emotionally attached to me. She had come to respect me as a man who believed in the righteousness of his cause, was willing to sacrifice his life for the freedom of the Vietnamese people, and was, at his core, a good and decent man. In other words: I had become, in Tu yen's emotional heart, an American version of Van. Had Van realized this, he would have personally tortured and killed me in the same manner he had Hu'ng.

I spent the week doing my menial paper work but continued to investigate what it would take to marry Tuyen and sponsor her and her family into the United States. To begin the process, there would have to be a complete and thorough investigation into her background, interviews of her family and friends, and no evidence discovered of Communist affiliations in her past. I quickly realized that this process would take an enormous amount of time and effort. In my naivete, I saw no hindrance to this process, as I felt confident that the background check would hold no surprises as far as Tuyen was concerned.

I determined that since I had extended my enlistment two years, the best means of accomplishing my goal was to stay in Vietnam for the remaining two years of my enlistment and fight through the system in order to marry Tuyen and bring her to the United States. I even contemplated staying in Vietnam after my enlistment was over and becoming a permanent expatriate. I would risk everything to spend the rest of my life with her.

By the time of our next rendezvous, I had put together a plan that I was sure would convince her of the viability of our future together. I arrived at the restaurant a half-hour early, as usual. Sitting at our favorite table, I contemplated how this date was the most important one of our relationship.

Two Viet Cong agents observed my arrival from across the street, while a third agent—a suicide bomber—approached me. When the assassin was five feet away and just about to terminate the life of everyone in the immediate vicinity, a waiter passed between us. The assassin, focused on his mission, proceeded to detonate the bomb attached to his chest. A tremendous explosion shook the place, and, although I was partially shielded from the lethal blast's effects, I was blown from my chair, knocked unconscious, and wounded by shards of glass and shrapnel.

Tuyen was a block away from the restaurant when she heard the explosion and rushed to the site. She saw many killed and wounded before finally finding me—unconscious and a bloody mess. Tuyen did what she could for me, making sure I was one of the first victims rushed to the military hospital.

I'd been unconscious for twenty-four hours, and Tuyen was by my side when I awoke. I had no memory of either being in the restaurant or of the blast. I had suffered a concussion and numerous cuts and abrasions but was otherwise very fortunate. The explosion appeared to all to be a random act of violence not directly intended for me.

Everyone believed this to be true—except for Tuyen, who knew instinctively that Van was behind the attack. This knowledge filled her with fear, apprehension, and guilt. She knew that the information she had passed on to Colonel Khan and Van of my claims about the coming attack had almost resulted in my death. This act of terror left her with an empty feeling and a need to reevaluate her outlook on the world in general.

I stayed in the hospital for two days with Tuyen by my side. During this time, we each realized how lucky I had been and she could not help but fall deeper in love with me. I was no longer just a sexual toy and conduit of information. Van was still the love of her life, and the Communist cause enveloped her, but I had pierced Tuyen's emotional armor. When I returned to duty after two days, we were more tightly bound than ever.

CHAPTER

18

Colonel Khan was well satisfied with the arrangements for the coming offensive. Behind the scenes, he had stashed enough money in a Swiss bank to ensure he would live in the lap of luxury for the rest of his life. It didn't matter to him who won the coming offensive, as he had made plans for his removal from the country any time he gave the command. Pilots had been bribed, and a jet was at his beck and call at Bien Hoa Airport outside Saigon.

He had not seen his family in months, and this didn't bother him in the least. He looked forward to leaving the country with only one person, and the person he had chosen was Tuyen. She was aware of the attention Colonel Khan had given her since they had met and been sexually intimate. The result was that he believed she was his for the taking. Colonel Khan had no inkling of the dedication and love that Tuyen had for Van.

The Colonel had to concentrate on coordinating the various units in his area of command as to the timing of the coming offensive. The Communist High Command had decided that the offensive would be kicked off in the early morning hours of the beginning of the TET holidays of 1968. The reasoning behind this was that tradition called for a cease-fire then. The majority of ARVN troops returned to their homes during this period, leaving a skeleton force defending the major bases in South Vietnam.

The American command placed all troops in defensive positions throughout the country. The attacks continued at Khe San and Dak To with more and more Allied troops being committed to these battles and both sides suffering horrific casualties. The Communist High Command felt these losses were well worth it, since they were achieving their purpose of drawing the Allied forces in quantity into these two major battles at the expense of defending the rest of the country. As a result of these engagements, the Allied forces became careless. Colonel Khan's immediate concern was ensuring that all area commanders had their troops ready in case the attack date changed.

The heaviest attacks occurred at Khe Sahn on January 21 after a continuous buildup of Communist troops during the preceding month. All our land supply routes had been severed, leaving the only means of resupply airborne. This achieved the first phase of the Communist attack, limiting the supplies available to the Allied forces and using the monsoon season to their advantage, as it limited the flying time for resupply. The Communists had overrun the outpost of Lang Vei, a mile from Khe Sahn , by the end of the year. The Marines were forced to live like rats underground, scurrying out as supplies arrived, constantly wet, lacking sleep, and terrified. We dropped Forty thousand bombs weighing twenty thousand tons each right up to the perimeter of Khe Sahn during the month of January and still the Communists attacked.

The Marines hunkered down in a defensive perimeter and inflicted horrible casualties on the NVA. Six thousand Marines withstood everything the Communists threw at them. Another Dien Bien Phu had been avoided. The attack at Dak To started in early October and continued through January. Khe Sahn's adjacency to Cambodia made it easy for the Communists to beat up the Allied forces, retreat to Cambodia for resupply and replacement of their killed and wounded, and return to the battlefield. Elements of the Fourth Infantry Division, One Hundred Seventy

Third Airborne Division, and numerous ARVN units had been committed to the battle, and this was exactly what the Communists wanted: the commitment of Allied troops to Khe Sahn and Dak To, drawing these troops from the rest of the country.

Dak To became reminiscent of Korea; as the Allies captured hilltop after hilltop, the Communists retreated to Cambodia, the Allies abandoned the hill, and the Communists returned to fight another day. Once large numbers of Allied troops had been tied down at Dak To, the Communists continued harassing them while preparing for the TET offensive. Over half the Allied forces had been committed to Dak To and Khe Sahn. The stage has been set for an event that would alter the outcome of the war.

Colonel Khan believed he had only one aspect of his planned escape to finalize: ensuring that Tuyen agreed with his plan. He traveled to My Tho under his cover as a Buddhist monk, checking on local cadre along the way as to their preparations and readiness. He was pleased to find all participants in a high state of readiness, chomping at the bit to launch the offensive. He sent word to Tuyen that he would meet her at the villa, where they would spend the night.

Having just returned from her visit with Van and renewed her vows with him, Tuyen was in a state of emotional strain. Colonel Khan arrived in a state of anticipation and enjoyed a long, relaxing day, relishing Tuyen's physical and emotional charms. During the course of their conversation, Colonel Khan revealed his plan to flee the country no matter who was in control at the end of the offensive and his desire that Tuyen accompany him.

She knew that this was an impossibility due to her commitment to the Communist cause and Van, but she also realized that a man of Colonel Khan's importance would not take no for an answer. Tuyen asserted that she could not abandon her family, and Colonel Khan assured her that arrangements had been made for them to escape also. She appeared to go along with the escape plan in order to inform Van of Colonel Khan's plans. She knew that Colonel Khan had no intention of bringing her family out of Vietnam and would ultimately assassinate them. Tuyen acted as if she was thrilled with his plan, and Colonel Khan left filled with confidence that their future was unfolding as it should.

As soon as Colonel Khan departed, Tuyen sent word to Van through a trusted friend that they must meet concerning Colonel Khan. This was difficult, as Van was in the midst of final preparations for the coming offensive and needed to be focused and available to his cadre. They arranged to meet at a small village in the Plain of Reeds, which was controlled by the Viet Cong and safe for all involved.

They were together within two days, and Tuyen informed Van of Colonel Khan's Swiss bank account and his plan to escape to Paris no matter who was victorious in the TET offensive. She then told Van of Colonel Khan's intent to have her leave the country with him.

Van became enraged by Colonel Khan's intent to abandon the Communist cause in order to benefit himself. He was also more than jealous of Colonel Khan's designs on Tuyen. If Colonel Khan had been in the room, Van would have killed him.

Eventually, Tuyen calmed him, pointing out that Colonel Khan was a very powerful man, and that any charges made against him would be difficult to prove. It would only be Tu yen's word against his. In addition, with the offensive so close, Colonel Khan's position necessitated his command of his troops, and the offensive would require all the expertise the Viet Cong had at their disposal.

Van assured Tuyen that he would not allow her to be whisked away by Colonel Khan and that after the Communist victory, he would take care of the situation. Since Van knew that Colonel Khan had no intention of whisking Tuyen's family out of the country, he reassured her that he would make arrangements for them to be sent to Cambodia as soon as possible.

Tuyen left the meeting feeling confident that no matter what happened, she and her family's future was secure under Van's guidance. Van returned to his preparations for the coming offensive, and Tuyen returned to her duties as a spy.

CHAPTER
19

My continued espousal of my theory of a coming attack alarmed my superior officer. Captain Donaldson had been in My Tho for eighteen months and felt he was the lead intelligence expert in the area. In addition to his intelligence duties, he had spearheaded the pacification movement and was quite proud of what he viewed as its success. A college graduate, he'd gone to Officers Candidate School and proceeded up the ranks. He had no combat experience but, having majored in psychology, felt that he had mastered the Asian mind.

Captain Donaldson was the epitome of the "ugly American;" he viewed all Asians as fools. He had no concept of how the average Vietnamese saw the world, nor did he care. This same attitude applied to military personnel, so there was no way Captain Donaldson could view any opinion I expressed as having any value. His greatest skill was as a meticulous investigator, and this had served him well in his duties as an intelligence officer. He held no regard for my theories and was insulted by the fact that I had dared to believe that I might have a better insight into what the enemy was planning than highly trained intelligence officers. As a result, Captain Donaldson decided to look into my day-to-day activities, hoping to catch me in some type of activity that might land me in the stockade.

Captain Donaldson commenced surveillance on me and was surprised to discover very quickly that I had established a relationship with Tuyen, who he learned worked at the local PX and volunteered at the hospital. After a month of surveillance and learning of my inquiries into how to marry a Vietnamese, he became convinced that this relationship was very foolhardy for any American serviceman, much less anyone working in an intelligence unit. The captain didn't confront me because he first needed more information concerning who Tuyen was and what her background entailed.

The initial report he received back aroused his suspicions. She seemed to have appeared from nowhere three months previously and begun working at the PX. She spoke very good English and appeared to be well educated and worldly. Captain Donaldson was determined to get to the location of her origins. He had some of her coworkers approached by loyal South Vietnamese agents, who made inquiries into her background. Learning that she and I had met several times a month at a lavish villa far beyond her means aroused his suspicions further. It had become obvious we were having a love affair in opulent surroundings that neither of us could afford.

Upon further inquiry, he discovered that the villa was owned by Comrade Long, who Tuyen represented as her aunt. It was interesting that her aunt made her villa available to Tuyen for her amorous meetings with me, yet Tuyen spent every other evening in a crowded apartment with her roommates. Further investigation of Comrade Long revealed that she was a woman of mystery who appeared to have a great deal of money of which there was no discernable source. Captain Donaldson decided to bring her in for questioning.

Comrade Long was very convincing in the tale she wove. She explained that she was the daughter of a wealthy plantation owner who had passed on in the early sixties, and, because of extensive damage to the rubber plantation by American artillery, her father had been compensated by the United States Government for its destruction. Upon her father's death, Comrade Long was made the sole heir to the estate. She readily gave references to be checked by the authorities and was released with the advice that she was subject to further questioning.

She immediately contacted Colonel Khan and informed him of the inquiry. Colonel Khan was not concerned because he knew the convoluted workings of the Vietnamese social fabric would result in great delays of any inquiry into anyone's background. Since the coming offensive would be triggered within a month, any inquiry begun now would be fruitless. Colonel Khan ordered Comrade Long to allow Tuyen to continue her liaisons in order to squeeze as much information as possible from me.

I was surprised when my job was eliminated. Told to report to Captain Donaldson, I thought my orders to return home had come through. Since I had decided to extend my tour in Vietnam, I felt that this would be an appropriate time to express this desire.

Upon reporting to Captain Donaldson, I was stunned to discover that that the captain was aware of my relationship with Tuyen and had made inquiries into her background. It quickly became apparent that he had done his homework and was informed as to the extent of our relationship and where our love nest was and was aware of my inquiries into marrying a Vietnamese national. Captain Donaldson spoke of Comrade Long's providing the villa we used as our love nest and inquired as to the possibility of both of us being Communist agents.

I was astounded by Captain Donaldson's inquiry into my personal life and even more shocked at the accusation that Tuyen could be a Communist agent. Captain Donaldson wanted to know the status of my relationship with Tuyen, what I may have told her about my work, and what I might know about her background.

Knowing better than to reveal any of the conversations I'd had with Tuyen about my work or our conversations about my belief that there was a Communist offensive in the works, I only spoke of my love for Tuyen and desire to marry her. I detailed how I'd initially met her at the PX and how she cared for me after I had been wounded. I spoke of our growing love for each other and revealed that she had family in a town in the northern Mekong Delta, where her father had owned a rubber plantation, which he'd lost to the Communists. I explained that he had died of grief, prompting Tuyen to move to My Tho to start a new life.

Captain Donaldson wanted to know what I knew about Comrade Long, and I truthfully replied that she was Tuyen's aunt and I had only met her one time. He then wanted to know if I hadn't wondered as to where Tuyen had made the connections to be able to use the villa, and I replied that I had been told by Tuyen that that she had a wealthy aunt who allowed us to use it, and I had accepted this statement at face value. Captain Donaldson also asked if I hadn't found it strange that when the terrorist bomb exploded, Tuyen was two blocks away, and I had only been there at her request.

The inference was clear that Tuyen was a Communist agent and had set me up. I was furious at this suggestion and maintained my certainty that she fully supported the Allied cause and hated the Communists. Captain Donaldson then asked me if I had mentioned the supposed turncoat Hu'ng to Tuyen. I insisted that I had never discussed my work with her but trusted her fully.

I was told to report back to my barracks and remain there under informal restriction until more could be found out about Tuyen's background. I left the meeting somewhat shaken, having second thoughts about the coincidences the captain had brought up about Tuyen and totally confused as to what the future might bring. Captain Donaldson had inferred that I might not be allowed to leave Vietnam until her background had been checked.

I had plenty of time on my hands when I returned to my barracks. My trust in Tuyen was unshaken, and my love for her had not waned. My suspicions were directed toward the American military and Captain Donaldson. I had been on the wrong side of the captain ever since I had finagled my way on to the SOG mission. I believed that the captain had read more into Tuyen's activities than was warranted, and I still viewed her as a beautiful, sophisticated Vietnamese lady with whom I wished to spend the rest of my life.

It would take absolute proof to shake my commitment to Tuyen.

CHAPTER
20

After Van's rendezvous with Tuyen, he returned to his Cambodian sanctuary and immediately sent his most trusted agents to look at Colonel Khan's most recent activities. Needing substantial evidence of Tuyen's accusations, he instructed his agents to look into any bribery activity that pointed to Colonel Khan, including any influence peddling he may have been involved in. It would be impossible to pinpoint any Swiss bank accounts without raising suspicions. However, Colonel Khan had alienated enough of the younger Communist cadre with his authoritarian manner that is should be easy to reveal a great deal of money laundering and influence peddling.

Van's agents returned shortly with definitive proof that that the colonel had an organized shakedown scheme whereby all merchants and farmers involved in trade in the Mekong Delta had been paying a protection fee to Colonel Khan. Although the fee was not great, when multiplied by the number of extorted over the course of five years, it amounted to millions.

Several officers promoted by Colonel Khan had also paid large fees to achieve their rank. This had not applied to Van, as he had no money to pay and was such an invaluable asset to Colonel Khan that he was not forced to pay. Besides, it was obvious that Van's dedication to the principles of the revolution would not allow for any corruption. Van determined that Colonel Khan would have to be eliminated after the victorious offensive, not only because of Van's personal feelings but also because of his corruptive influence within the cause.

Van became determined to eliminate Colonel Khan personally. Once the offensive was underway, he would have the freedom to travel at will. Van was determined to cleanse the party of corruption, even if he remained as the only party member. The elimination of Colonel Khan would also ensure Tuyen's safety. He epitomized everything that Van had been fighting to eliminate all these years. The knowledge that there were Viet Cong cadre who acted no differently than the corrupt South Vietnamese enraged Van. There would be a purge when the war was won.

It was now mid-January 1968. All was in readiness for the coming offensive. Only a traitor could threaten the events about to unfold, and Van had ensured that his forces were well aware of what happened to traitors.

Van was vibrating with anticipation about the coming assault, which would ensure the Communist cause a future in South Vietnam, allow Van to eliminate both me and Colonel Khan, and allow Van and Tuyen to move forward in their commitment to the Communist cause and each other.

Colonel Khan was looking forward to the coming offensive for different reasons, because of his arrangements to flee the country to his hideaway and because he was confident that Tuyen would accompany him.

I was only aware of my love of Tuyen and was concerned that Captain Donaldson's investigation into her past would jeopardize our plans to marry and remain in Vietnam.

Tuyen was unaware of any investigation into her background; she only knew that the offensive was coming soon, that she would be permanently joined with Van, and that the Communist cause would be victorious. Tuyen realized that her relationship with me would have to end. She only hoped that I would leave the country unharmed before the offensive began. As for Colonel Khan, she despised him and everything he stood for and felt confident that Van would take care of the situation when the time came.

With one week left before the TET holiday, and not knowing when or if my orders would be issued allowing me to leave Vietnam, I was in a quandary as to how to go about requesting to extend my tour. If I could not, I would go AWOL and disappear into the anonymity of Saigon. I would do whatever it took to remain with Tuyen for the rest of my life.

I visited her at the PX and indicated that we must meet at the villa the coming weekend. I decided that I would not reveal to her that her background was being investigated by Captain Donaldson, indicating only that my orders to return home were imminent. I was determined to somehow get my orders changed so that I could remain in Vietnam. I believed implicitly in Tuyen's loyalty to the Allied cause and thought if we could join our futures together, our souls will be complete.

I devised a means of being absent from the barracks for several days: bribing the officer of the day to report me as present. The only way my absence would be detected would be if Captain Donaldson demanded my presence, which was highly unlikely on the weekend, and at this point, I didn't really care if I was caught.

I met Tuyen at the villa, and it was a joyous meeting for both of us. I welcomed the attention she showered upon me, and Tuyen, knowing that this would be the last time we would be together, was enveloped in a sense of serendipity at life's whims. She made sure that my every wish was fulfilled and lavished me with every sensual pleasure known to the female mind.

I absorbed these sensual pleasures at great length, knowing that my departure may be imminent and having no idea when I might return. All I knew was that I loved Tuyen more than anything on earth, and if I could not have a future with her, I had not much reason to live.

Tuyen focused on the moment, agreeing with all of my plans for the future while in her heart knowing that her future lay with

Van and the cause of Communism. Having developed the ability to separate her love of me from her commitment to Van as merely an obedience to orders , she felt no remorse for her duplicity. Tuyen's emotional involvement took a backseat to her commitment to the cause, and her love of Van superseded everything else. Her only wish was that I return to the United States prior to the coming offensive. When this was accomplished, Tuyen would disappear into the loving arms of Communism, and she hoped I would think she had been destroyed by the war.

We spent the remainder of the weekend at the villa parting on a note of expectation, each for a different reason and with very different expectations.

CHAPTER
21

Historically, the TET holidays were one of joyous revelry and celebration for the Vietnamese. A time of doing away with the old year and welcoming the new, it lasted for three days and was heavily dosed with religious observations—but also with plenty of time for sensual exploration. For as long as the Vietnamese had been at war with the Chinese, the French, and the Americans, TET had been a time of peace with each side observing a cease-fire out of their respect for worthy opponents and the religious meaning of the holiday. There were various breakdowns of the three-day truce, but always on a limited basis, just to keep everyone honest.

TET 1968 would prove an exception to the rule. Colonel Khan was operating on a short fuse, anticipating the offensive and making sure that all his units in the Mekong Delta were ready to start the attack in unison. Thousands of troops had infiltrated all the major cities of Vietnam in preparation for the coming offensive, stockpiling arms and supplies around the cities to be attacked. There had been no indication of any Allied knowledge of what was about to envelop the country: no leaves cancelled and no extraordinary defensive preparations being made. The cities of Hue, Saigon, My Tho, and Can Tho were primary targets of the offensive.

With intricate plans in place to flee his headquarters in Saigon, rendezvous with Tuyen, and escape to a safe sanctuary where his stolen wealth would provide him with a life of luxury, Colonel Khan was ready for the offensive.

I spent my time restricted to the barracks planning how I could remain in Vietnam, or, if forced to return to the United States, how I could return quickly. Through contacts I had at headquarters, I had discovered that my orders to return home had been issued, only to be held up by Captain Donaldson until the investigation into Tu yen's background had been finished. I decided that if my orders to return home had not been issued after TET, I would request an extension of my tour of duty in Vietnam. Since I had done nothing wrong and was confident that Tuyen was innocent of any charges, I would go over Captain Donaldson's head if needed and demand action.

Van had proceeded from his refuge in Cambodia in order to have better control of his troops' attack throughout the Mekong Delta. He had fifty thousand troops at his disposal, all hard core and well supplied. Van envisioned the entire Mekong Delta being within his control in a matter of days. He had positioned himself so as to be in close proximity to Tuyen's location in order to protect her during the offensive and to thwart any efforts by Colonel Khan to kidnap her. He had made sure that Tuyen's family was safely in Cambodia. Van was at the apex of his capabilities and could feel the call of destiny.

Khe Sahn continued to be the site of a prolonged siege. The North Vietnamese rained artillery shells on the six thousand Marines dug into their positions. Sappers attempted to breach the barbed wire of the compound nightly, and there was no such thing as a break in the action. The weather did not cooperate, limiting resupply of the base. As all land routes had been cut, the beleaguered occupants were on short rations. It was more important to deliver ammunition than food and water.

The Allies were under the impression that the intent of the North Vietnamese was to turn Khe Sanh into another Dien Bien

Phu, whereas in reality, the North Vietnamese were content to draw more and more Allied troops into the battle. Dak To was a continuing flow of troops on both sides up and down the mountain. The Allies assaulted the dug-in North Vietnamese positions, suffered atrocious casualties, conquered their objectives, and moved on. The North Vietnamese retreated into Cambodia, resupplied, and returned to the fray. We were committing an increasing number of Allied troops to the battle, just as the North Vietnamese desired.

January 29 dawned in the city of Hue to a mood of religious and social expectation. As due its position as the religious and political center of South Vietnam, Hue was central to the cause of Democratic freedom in Vietnam and looked upon as a bastion of liberal thought and political activism. Approximately 20 percent of the city's population was Catholic, as it was one of the few metropolises in South Vietnam that had an open attitude toward religious freedom. The brother of the one-time president of South Vietnam, Ngo Din Diem, had been the Catholic Archbishop of Hue in the early sixties. Given that the majority of Vietnamese were Buddhist and the current regime Catholic, the city of Hue held a unique position in Vietnamese society.

The truce put into effect for the TET lunar New Year celebration had the population in a festive mood. Beautiful young Vietnamese girls wandered the streets of Hue, shopping in preparation for the coming holiday. Seventy percent of South Vietnamese soldiers returned to their home villages to celebrate the holidays, and all allied forces were on a stand-down close to their major base camps.

Thirty percent of Allied troops had been moved into the Central Highlands. The Fourth Infantry Division, the 173rd Airborne, the 101st Airborne, and the Marines at Khe Sahn were all located in the north of South Vietnam, limiting defensive capabilities in the rest of the country. The Allied forces had placed themselves in a position of great vulnerability.

The city of Saigon was calm, believing in the future of the South Vietnamese government and placing itself in the hands of the United States Military. Peace appeared to be on the horizon through the hamlet pacification program, and the majority of the citizenry basked in a false sense of security. In the Mekong Delta, farmers paused in their daily ritual of planting and harvesting, prayed for a fruitful season, and looked forward to a serene future. Even the water buffalo seemed lulled into a false sense of security.

That illusion was soon shattered. In the early morning hours of January 31, the Communists initiated simultaneous attacks on thirty-six hamlets, towns, and major cities. Allied forces were caught completely off guard because of the TET cease-fire. Satchel bombers blew the gates to the city of Hue off their hinges, and North Vietnamese troops poured in. The city was divided in two by the Perfume River with the Old Imperial City on the north side and the modern city of Hue to the south. It only took two hours for five thousand North Vietnamese troops to take control of both sides of the river, as there were no defenders on site.

The two areas that held out were the ARVN compound and the United States military compound. Fifty Marines were wounded in the Old City and retreated to the New City. Reinforcements were called in but only had access by water. Air strikes and artillery were banned by the South Vietnamese High Command so as not to destroy the ancient city. While in control, the North Vietnamese took advantage of the situation. Assassination squads spread throughout the city with lists of Catholics, intellectuals, liberals, and government officials to eliminate.

There were no Allied defenders at first. South Vietnamese troops reported back to their units under heavy enemy fire. Elements of the Twenty Fifth Infantry Division, the 196th Light Infantry Brigade, and the Second Marine Division responded to the attack with heavy weapons fire. Targets of the assassination squads took refuge in churches and political buildings in hopes of protection. As the Allied troops reorganized, fierce fighting continued within the city. It took twenty-four hours for the South Vietnamese army to get itself together, while the American forces did the majority of the fighting. Many Vietnamese became victims of the assassination squads. Once inside the City of Hue, the North Vietnamese assassins slaughtered over five thousand inhabitants and burned many buildings to the ground. Priests, nuns, and orphans were assassinated as if they were political opponents.

The North Vietnamese reveled in their atrocities, viewing all the residents of the city as supporters of the corrupt Saigon government and foes of Communism. They took no prisoners. Mass graves became standard operating procedure. By the third day of fighting, the Allies had regrouped enough to initiate offensive attacks. It was too late for many civilians. The war in the City of Hue had changed from guerilla theatre to conventional warfare, with fighting from building to building, block to block, hand to hand.

The decision was finally made to destroy the City of Hue in order to save it with artillery and air strikes. Helicopters strafed suspected enemy enclaves. The Communists used women and children as shields in an effort to avoid Allied fire and attacked, burned, and destroyed Red Cross facilities with screaming wounded inside. Slowly, hour by hour, the Allied forces stabilized the city. Progress was measured at one hundred yards per day. The Communists fought to the bitter end, delaying Allied incursions as the assassination squads finished their work and expanded their search for allied sympathizers. Fighting continued for three weeks before a nervous peace was established. The Communists had massacred upwards of six thousand civilians and wounded many more. Neither the City of Hue nor its occupants would ever be the same.

In Saigon, the initial attack came against the American Embassy and the Imperial Palace—two symbols of American decadence. Suicide squads gained entry into the American Embassy with the intent of killing everyone inside. Marine defenders fought off the assault, inflicting great casualties on the attackers and annihilating them, but not before reinforcements arrived. Gunships strafed the grounds of the embassy.

Attackers disguised as servants immediately occupied the Imperial Palace from within. Hand-to-hand fighting ensued. Elements of the First Infantry Division were called into the city to secure the embassy and the Imperial Palace. Fighting raged within the city, especially in the Chinese Cholon district, where Communists had stockpiled supplies and weapons. Assassination squads roamed the city, murdering perceived as an enemy of the Communists.

Fortunately, American and South Vietnamese troops were able to contain the attackers with the aid of gunships. Bien Hoa Airport, the main entry and exit point into South Vietnam, was under siege, resulting in troops preparing to depart for home being issued M-16 rifles and sent back into combat and arriving troops experiencing combat the moment they stepped off the plane. Long Bin Hospital was under attack, and mobile patients were armed in order to protect the more seriously wounded patients. Mortar attacks continued throughout the day and night.

After two days, the Allied forces had stabilized the situation but suffered for it. Communist suicide squads carried out atrocities just as they had in the city of Hue. The Communists paid a heavy price to delay the allied advances in order to destroy the inner structure of South Vietnamese society. As the battle continued, superior Allied air power proved decisive in containing the guerillas. The Viet Cong in the Saigon area sacrificed their cadre in order to inflict maximum casualties on the South Vietnamese. It had become apparent after a few days of fighting that the general uprising the Communists had anticipated in the south was not occurring, and as a result, the Communists decided to kill as many civilians as possible, the consensus being that my enemy's friend is my enemy. No one in the Communist High Command had reasoned that the average South Vietnamese preferred Democracy to Communism, resulting in a serious miscalculation by the Communist High Command.

The battle continued for another three weeks with the Allies slowly but surely weeding out the attackers. Every member of the Viet Cong was willing to sacrifice his life for the cause of Communism. As a result, the Viet Cong had ceased to exist as a fighting force by the time the offensive was quelled. In the Mekong Delta, all major cities and hamlets were under attack.

Containing two-thirds of the population of South Vietnam, the Delta had been heavily controlled by the Communists until the introduction of the Ninth Infantry Division Riverine force in early 1967. These soldiers lived on Navy barracks ships depending on the Navy to insert them into the Rung Sat saltwater enclave, a major supply and arms storage area for the Viet Cong, in early

1967. They could only operate in the mangrove swamps for three to five days at a time due to the fact that they were fighting in water.

By TET 1968, the troops of the Ninth Infantry Division had secured 50 percent of the Mekong Delta and the pacification program had become a huge success. All that the citizens of the Mekong Delta desired was peace and prosperity. The largest Viet Cong attacks occurred at My Tho and Can Tho, the major population centers and trade centers of the Mekong Delta.

Many South Vietnamese soldiers claimed the Mekong Delta as their home, and as a result of the TET stand-down, they were home with their families enjoying the holiday when the offensive began. They returned to their units within two days of the beginning of the offensive, but many were massacred in the process. Can Tho came under heavy attack from Communist forces during the first few days of fighting.

The arrival of the Riverine gun boats, named Monitors after the Civil War ironclads, changed everything. These gunboats were equipped with quad fifty machine guns and rapid-fire grenade launchers capable of firing hundreds of rounds per minute. They also had flamethrowers. Needless to say, when these units arrived on the scene, they saved the day. Unfortunately, many civilians had been assassinated by the Viet Cong by then. After two days of heavy fighting, the Allied forces had stabilized the situation. Fighting continued, but the cities and hamlets of the Mekong Delta had withstood the onslaught, although not without a heavy loss of lives.

CHAPTER
22

Colonel Khan was in Saigon when the fighting commenced. His command was in constant contact with all elements of the offensive in the Mekong Delta. The Colonel was not involved with the units attacking Saigon but obviously knew what was occurring. Initially, he was carried away by the euphoria of the initial successes of the Communist offensive, basking in wonder at the enormity and total surprise of it. Reports of the penetration of the United States Embassy and suicide squad attacks at the Bien Hoa Airport and Long Bin Hospital fed his enthusiasm. Reports from the main towns and hamlets of the Mekong Delta indicated that the element of surprise had allowed the Communist troops to occupy many locations. The lack of South Vietnamese troops on duty due to the TET holiday cease-fire had obviously played into the hands of the Communists.

But as several days passed, it became apparent that when the enormous firepower of the Mobile Riverine Force was brought to bear on the Communists, they had a devastating impact on the attackers. Within three days, the tide had turned and the Allied forces were in the process of pushing the attackers out of the towns and villages of the Mekong Delta. The general uprising of the local populace that the Communists had expected had not occurred here, nor anywhere else in South Vietnam.

Even without local support, the Communists' assassination squads had eliminated large numbers of intellectuals, Catholics, and political cadre throughout South Vietnam. This alone was worth the Communist casualties. Colonel Khan had directed his forces to press the attack in spite of all obstacles, taking advantage of the immensity of the offensive and causing as many casualties as possible.

Van was at the center of commanding the fighting in the Mekong Delta. Like everywhere else, his forces had the element of surprise in their favor. Major hamlets were overrun, and Can Tho and My Tho were under siege. However, after three days of fighting, the tide had turned. Viet Cong forces had been stalemated in Can Tho and My Tho. There had been no general uprising, and the general populace had been alienated by the atrocities committed by the Communist attackers.

Van's forces were taking horrible casualties and had no place to aid the wounded, as there was no way to get them to Cambodia. Many Communist attackers died of untreated wounds. Van's troops were in constant combat with the Riverine forces, and although he had numerical superiority, the tremendous firepower of the Riverines eventually drove his troops out of Can Tho and My Tho. Van was facing his opponent with a decimated army.

When the first wave of attacks hit My Tho, I grabbed my weapon and headed for one of the perimeter bunkers. All Allied troops were occupying defensive positions and poured heavy firepower at the Viet Cong attackers. The mass of Communist troops came in waves of infantry at Americans, only to be driven back by machine-gun fire, gunships, and the Riverine Monitors. The arrival of the Monitors with their quad fifties and automatic-fire grenade launchers held the Communists at bay. Still, assassination squads penetrated the city and performed their deadly mission. After three days, the city of My Tho was secure but at great cost.

Tuyen was in the hospital when the attack began. Because of the great number of casualties, she remained at her post where she saw the local citizenry brought in after being attacked by the Communist suicide squads. She was appalled by the number of casualties and the atrocities committed. The Communists constantly mortared the hospital and heavily damaged it. Units of the Ninth Infantry Division were brought in to defend the hospital and its patients. After three days of treating the wounded, the hospital was seriously low on blood and medical supplies. On the forth day, the fighting lessened and supplies began to trickle in, but they still had far more patients than they could handle.

Reports by the survivors confirmed the immensity of the assassinations of the civilian populace by the Communist attackers throughout the Mekong Delta. The wounded being brought into the hospital were more than 50 percent civilian, and many had been wounded by machetes. Entire families had been wiped out. It had become apparent that the if victory could not be achieved in the Mekong Delta, then the Communists would eliminate as many civilian supporters of the Allies as possible.

Tuyen knew that these atrocities were being committed under Van's orders, and the beginnings of disillusionment with both the Communist cause and Van began to fester in her heart. She remained on duty at the hospital for four days working virtually nonstop. Her worst nightmare would be to find Van or me as one of the casualties.

After four days of constant combat, Colonel Khan could see the writing on the wall. He was dead on his feet, but even in this condition, it had become apparent to him that that the offensive was failing. Even though the Communist forces had inflicted horrendous casualties on the South Vietnamese military and civilian populace, there had been no local uprising of the native populace and the Communist attackers had absorbed massive casualties for which there were no replacements. The Allied firepower had been so overwhelming that the Viet Cong had virtually ceased to exist as a fighting force.

Colonel Khan realized that he was better off out of the country in his safe haven with Tuyen, so he proceeded to implement his escape plan. He notified his escape crew at Bien Hoa Airport to be ready on a moment's notice to whisk he and his entourage out of

Vietnam. Colonel Khan could have left immediately save for the fact that he was determined to take Tuyen with him. He decided to rest and refresh his body and mind for a day and then travel to My Tho and collect her.

Van continued to push his troops onward. Despite having more than 60 percent of his command rendered nonexistent by death and wounds, his soldiers fought on, all clinging to the firm belief that their cause was just and any sacrifice was worth the expulsion of the Western devils and the overthrow of the Saigon government. Van had joined his troops in My Tho and was initially delighted with the results of the attack. The element of surprise had allowed his assassination squads to roam the Delta at will eliminating Allied sympathizers. The mainline Viet Cong were expendable as long as the assassination squads were successful.

What was becoming apparent to Van was that as his men were being eliminated, so was the future command structure in the Delta. This played right into the hands of the North Vietnamese High Command, who realized that the more Viet Cong eliminated during the offensive, the less elimination of the Viet Cong infrastructure would be necessary when they were victorious. The North Vietnamese High Command would be able to take control of the structure of the Viet Cong in the south and thus be in complete control of the Communist forces throughout South Vietnam. As the fighting continued and casualties mounted, Van ordered his remaining forces to retreat to their Cambodian sanctuaries where doctors and resupply awaited them. Van remained in My Tho, determined to rescue Tuyen and bring her with him to the safety of Cambodia.

After four days of manning a defensive bunker at My Tho, I could see that the tide had turned. Although suffering from the lack of all the items essential for human survival—rest, food, and water—I was driven by the need to locate Tuyen. I had no plans after locating her.

Captain Donaldson's called me to his office and informed me that my orders to return to the United States had been on his desk for three weeks but had been placed on hold due to the investigation into Tuyen's background. Since nothing had been discovered, and my insistence that a major Communist offensive was coming had proven correct, Captain Donaldson decided that my removal from the theatre of operation was the best choice of action. I was ordered to report to Bien Hoa Airport processing station in three days' time.

I returned to my barracks, collected the few personal belongings I had, and began to search for Tuyen. I first checked at the PX where she worked. It had been obliterated by mortar attacks. Next, I checked the hospital where she volunteered and was informed that she had left the day before after taking care of the wounded for four days. Then I checked with the girls she roomed with and was told she had come and gone, taking her belongings with her. Exhausted, I proceeded to the villa where we had met for our trysts.

After resting for twenty-four hours, Colonel Khan proceeded with his preparations for escape. His stolen money sat in safe accounts in Switzerland, and his escape group was awaiting his arrival at Bien Hoa Airport. He only needed to travel to My Tho, collect Tuyen, and go. He traveled to My Tho again under the guise of a Buddhist monk, arriving the next day. He proceeded to the villa after contacting Comrade Long, who informed him that she had heard from Tuyen and believed she was in hiding there.

Tuyen was there trying to make contact with Van. This was very difficult due to the chaos of the moment, but she finally made contact with one of Van's lieutenants, who was aware of their relationship, and he passed word on to Van that she would wait for him there. After having something to eat and getting some rest, Tuyen waited.

At about five in the evening, she heard a noise in the courtyard. Thinking it was Van, she open the door and was shocked to discover me in the entryway. Regaining her composure, she greeted me hesitantly. I took it to be her innate shyness, and we embraced with true happiness at seeing each other. I told her that I had received orders to return home in two days. She was happy for me and went along with my plan to return to Vietnam after my leave and spend the remainder of my enlistment there arranging for our marriage—and then spend the rest of our lives in the United States.

Tuyen's main concern was that Van would appear while I was still there, and God only knew what would happen then. She explained to me that she was returning to her home village in the morning to escape the chaos of My Tho and visit her family. I agreed with her plan, as it coincided with mine to report to the processing center as directed. We enjoyed a simple meal and immersed ourselves in a final night of lovemaking, which would have to sustain us a very long time—longer than I wanted to imagine. We reaffirmed our love for each other, true love on my part but only partially true on Tuyen's.

About ten o'clock that evening, Van snuck up to the villa and peeked through the window. He was enraged to see Tuyen and me wrapped in each other's arms, but realizing her mission, Van controlled himself. He made plans to wait for my departure in the morning and then ambush and kill me as he should have done months ago.

As dawn broke in My Tho, Colonel Khan approached the villa. Time was of the essence, as Colonel Khan and Tuyen had a long and dangerous journey to Bien Hoa Airport. The Colonel heard voices inside and realized she was not alone. Entering the front alcove, he saw Tuyen and me. Speaking in Vietnamese to Tuyen, Colonel Khan directed her to move away so he could assassinate me. Tuyen claimed I was a bystander and begged Colonel Khan not to shoot me. She moved away to buy time but then saw Colonel Khan reveal an AK-47 assault rifle and point it at me.

Just as he was about to fire, Van burst through the door and killed Colonel Khan. Tuyen pleaded with Van not to shoot me, as they needed to leave before Colonel Khan's guards became aware of what had happened. They escaped through a side door, and I stood there in a state of shock at what had transpired.

I staggered out through the entryway and fled into the chaos of the streets of My Tho. I found my way back to the barracks and attempted to make sense of what had just occurred. It was apparent that the Vietnamese with whom Tuyen had escaped was a Viet Cong whom she was familiar with. It was also obvious that she had saved my life by stopping this person from killing me. The identity of the Buddhist monk with the AK-47 who had apparently wished to kill everyone was a mystery. After considering the events, I concluded that Tuyen was in fact a Communist spy in league with the Viet Cong she'd escaped with. I believed that she had affection for me, as proven by her saving my life, but she obviously had a stronger tie to the Viet Cong and the man she had escaped with.

My plans for the future now vanished, I became immersed in a fog of hatred for Tuyen, everything Vietnamese, and the war effort in general. I had spent the last year of my life fighting for a worthless cause, a worthless country, and a worthless ideal. I faded into a restless sleep, unable to absorb everything that had occurred in the last twenty-four hours. Awakening around noon, I showered and had something to eat. Then I found a deuce and a half truck heading for Bien Hoa Airport.

I arrived around dusk, found the area where I was to report for my return home, and collapsed into a deep sleep. When I awoke, I reported to the processing center, where my belongings were searched and I was assigned to a tent where I would await my departure to the land of the big PX in twenty-four hours. I was still in a state of shock, far removed from the euphoria my fellow travelers were enjoying.

CHAPTER

23

Colonel Khan's body was discovered by his guards, and his men conducted an intensive search was conducted for Tuyen and Van, who were seen escaping through the side door. With the number of refugees flooding the streets of My Tho, they had escaped into the mist. No one had seen me leave, so Colonel Khan's aide de camp came up with a story that, at great risk to himself, Colonel Khan was meeting with major subordinates about future Viet Cong operations in the Delta and was attacked by a group of ARVN troops. By sacrificing his own life, Colonel Khan had allowed his compatriots to escape from the ambush. Needing heroes to motivate future cadre, the myth of Colonel Khan's bravery made him the Davy Crockett of the TET offensive, and his wife and sons basked in the glory of his actions for the remainder of their lives. History has a habit of making heroes out of traitors.

Van guided Tuyen to his waiting entourage of committed cadre. Both were in a high state of anxiety, realizing that only the first phase of their escape to Cambodia had begun. Quickly changing from the black pajamas that Van was wearing and the upscale dress that Tuyen had worn, they took on the persona of refugees attempting to return to their farm in the Plain of Reeds. There had been no conversation between the two of them, as survival had become the mission of the day and both were exhausted.

Placing their future in the hands of his trusted aids, Van and Tuyen fought the need to sleep and slowly made their way to Cambodia, traveling at night to avoid Allied patrols. When they finally slept, Van dreamt of the ultimate victory of the cause while Tuyen had dreams of her future with Van—and also of a blurred future with me. Van slept more deeply than Tuyen.

I awoke to a day I had looked forward to for a year and continued to contemplate the events of the day before, literally burying the fact that Tuyen had always been a Communist spy with ties to the Viet Cong with whom she'd escaped. I concentrated on the fact that she had saved my life and therefore must love me. This raised my spirits, and by the time I boarded the plane to return home, I had decided to continue with my plan to spend the last two years of my enlistment searching for Tuyen and convincing her of my love. I knew it would not be easy to change her belief in the advantages of Communism over Democracy for her country, but I was convinced that her love for me existed, and the actions of the Communists over the last few days had to have had an effect on her outlook.

The twenty-hour flight home gave me plenty of time to plan my actions once I arrived home. I would have to deal with Jeri, who I had great affection for but nothing like the overwhelming love I felt for Tuyen. I had to find a way to break the news to Jeri that I had changed my mind and my future lay in the Far East without her. It would be easier to deal with my parents, coming up with a story that the military had ordered me back to Vietnam because of my intelligence expertise. They would be proud of me and would still believe I would return after my enlistment to the small town life I once left behind.

Upon arrival in Oakland, I processed through the usual military procedures and headed to the gate to catch my flight home. I was immediately accosted by peace protesters calling me and my companions baby killers and warmongers. I wasn't shocked by the peace protesters, but I was shocked by their number. What had happened to my country? When I'd left a year earlier, everything was "Rah, rah, rah! Beat the Communists!" Now it appeared that the tide of public opinion had turned against the war, and I and the rest of the military were being portrayed as bloodthirsty animals. By the time I took my seat on the plane, I was quite happy to leave California and return home to the Midwest.

I phoned Jeri upon my arrival in California, and she broke down in tears of happiness and agreed to meet me at the airport when I landed in Chicago. I was glad to hear her voice and looked forward to seeing her and my family.

I tried to make conversation with the businessman sitting next to me, but it became immediately apparent that this gentleman viewed me as an animal and had no desire for conversation. I resorted to reading the newspaper and was further shocked to read reports that the Communists were victorious in their TET offensive, which was totally opposed to what I had observed. I decided I had to put all these negative perspectives aside and enjoy my return to civilization.

Jeri was waiting for me with open arms, and we proceeded to my family home, where my parents, sister, uncles, and cousins welcomed me back enthusiastically. I was smothered with goodwill in the manner I'd expected, and although Jeri was constantly by my side, we had little time to talk. I retreated to my old room and fell into a deep, dreamless sleep. I needed a good rest in order to face the decisions I ultimately had to make.

Upon awakening, I had a Midwestern breakfast, lounged around the house, and quickly realized that although my body was home, my mind and spirit were still in Vietnam. I was due to report to Fort Hood, Texas, in thirty days. In the meantime, I needed to prepare my family for the idea that I intended to return to Vietnam. I also needed to break the news to Jeri that our relationship was at an end, not due to anything she had done but due to the fact that I was a different person than when I left home a year ago. My mind and heart were now dedicated to the future of Vietnam. I wouldn't mention that my return to Vietnam was solely for the purpose of locating Tuyen and determining whether she was or was not in love with me.

I had accepted that there was a distinct possibility that she was a Communist spy, but I was also convinced that her actions in the last moments of our meeting betrayed a deep emotional bond that I was convinced I could somehow cultivate. Obviously, I was blinded by love and disbelief that the love of my life could possibly be a Communist spy. I was sure that, due to her basic goodness, she would not continue to support the Communists once she understood how they operated and the tactics they employed.

Jeri had dropped out of college during the year I had been gone and was working at a computer company as a trainee. This at least relieved me of having to be with her most of the day but also left me with a lot of time on my hands. The constant newspaper and television reports of the success of the Communists during the TET offensive really demoralized me, as I had witnessed the decimation of the Viet Cong as a fighting force. As my days at home stretched on, I became aware of the popular opinion, even in my conservative Midwestern hometown, that the Vietnam War was a waste of time and that America should withdraw. Add to that the snide remarks about baby killers and atrocities, and all this made me want to remain in the United States no longer than necessary.

The depression these sentiments led to caused me to drink away most of the day, canceling several dates with Jeri and bringing great concern to my family. After two weeks of this behavior, Jeri had enough and confronted me about our relationship. She explained that she realized that I had been through a lot and was willing to see our relationship through this adjustment period, but only if we became engaged and made plans for the future.

This was just the opening I had been looking for. For the first, I revealed to her that I really had more than two years left on my enlistment. Jeri was shocked by this fact and felt left out of the equation, since I hadn't consulted her when I'd made the decision. She could see no way to withstand two more years of separation. Her bottom line was that the only way the relationship could continue was for us to marry now and be together no matter where I was stationed.

I knew that was an emotional impossibility for me. After three weeks of my drinking, my father insisted on a face-to-face meeting about my behavior and future plans. My father had been in World War II in the Infantry and therefore had some idea as to what I was going through mentally and emotionally. I was thankful for someone to confide in, as I felt as if I was going to explode.

I revealed everything to my father: what I'd experienced in combat, my love affair with Tuyen, and my plan to marry and spend the rest of my life with her. I described our final moments together and the horrible possibility that she was a Communist spy in love with a prominent Viet Cong. I explained that I still believed that Tuyen was a good person and that I intended to return to Vietnam for the rest of my tour, find her, and convince her of the evils of Communism.

My father pointed out that I would be risking my entire future in the United States for the love of Tuyen, but I explained that my entire outlook on life had changed because of my experiences in Vietnam, that I no longer had a Western outlook on life, and that I couldn't continue to live without Tuyen.

Fortunately, my father agreed that I must follow my heart and dreams wherever they may lead me, because if I didn't, I would regret it the rest of my life and wonder what could have been. My father didn't say it, but it was apparent that, because he adhered to the principle of doing what was correct and responsible, he had a great deal of regret about the decisions he had made as a young man.

I spent the remaining week of my leave sobering up and getting my affairs in order. I didn't see Jeri again, and my father was the only one who knew of my plans.

CHAPTER

24

Immediately upon arrival at Fort Hood, Texas, I was informed that if I returned at once to Vietnam, I would return as an infantryman. But if I wished to return to an intelligence unit, it would take some time. No way did I desire to return to the infantry, so I reported to my assigned intelligence unit in the Second Armored Division, where I reasserted my desire to return to Vietnam. Since my MOS was in intelligence, I was assigned to the main intelligence group of the Second Armored Division.

After a few days' indoctrination, it became apparent that this was a unit with no job. Daily routine consisted of company formation, breakfast, close-arms drill, lunch, and boredom. I quickly realized that nothing would happen to my request for transfer back to Vietnam unless I pushed the process.

I decided to infiltrate the main team in charge of dispensing orders at Division Headquarters, where all transfer orders were cut for the division. This was quite simple, as I took on the task of picking up any correspondence from the headquarters unit every day and got to know the clerks assigned there. Soon I was meeting several of these clerks at the local beer hall and determined who could help me in my quest for transfer. I discovered that two men handled all requests for assignment to Vietnam, and, due to the necessary structure of military life, they paid no attention to requests for these transfers, as this entailed a divergence from normal routine and required extra work, which everyone tried to avoid.

After a month of greasing the wheels with these clerks, I revealed my desire to return to Vietnam in an intelligence unit. I knew that my working knowledge of the Vietnamese language and experience in intelligence were in great demand in Vietnam. One clerk had no interest in helping me, but a second clerk made it apparent that he would be willing to assist me in my quest for the sum of two hundred fifty dollars. This was a great deal of money in 1968, but I was willing to spend anything to continue my search for Tuyen.

I agreed to the deal, but only if I could see a list of units handling intelligence in Saigon and determine where I wanted to be assigned. It didn't take me long to determine the unit I wished to be assigned to. I knew that if I was patient, I would be able to get an assignment to My Tho, where I would have access to captured documents and prisoners of war who would be able to help locate Tuyen.

My next mission was to discover who her Viet Cong lover was, but I was impatient. The clerk who had agreed to help me for a bribe informed me that an opening had come up in the unit I wished to be assigned to, but the report about my relationship with Tuyen, and the investigation into her background and the possibility that she may have been a Communist spy, barred my assignment to it. The clerk claimed that for another two hundred fifty dollars, the report could be deleted and I would have my dream assignment. Although it would take everything I had saved, I agreed. Anything was worth finding Tuyen. Within a few weeks, my orders arrived for assignment to Saigon and I prepared for the next chapter in my life.

Tuyen and Van made their way slowly toward the Cambodian border as the TET offensive wound down. Disguised as Buddhist monks, they and their entourage were afforded little attention, as there was such great chaos in the countryside. The ARVN forces concentrated on defensive positions, and the Americans concentrated on routing out the Viet Cong from My Tho and Can Tho, leaving the provinces to their own devices. They conducted the journey in total silence except for whispered communications as Van and Tuyen receded into a fog of weariness and shock at the events of the preceding days.

Tuyen felt no remorse for the demise of Colonel Khan, as she believed in her heart that he had received what he'd deserved. Her main concern was for me; she felt great sorrow that I had learned of her Communist commitment. She was shocked by the feelings she still had for me, not anything that could be termed love but a sense of responsibility and caring that was normally reserved for a brother. Tuyen hoped in her heart of hearts that I had survived the horror of the offensive and was now back in the United States. She knew that her memory of me would never leave her, and she felt a great deal of guilt at her duplicity and the pain she had caused me.

Tuyen's main concern now was to regain her strength through sleep, communicate with Van, plan their future together, and reunite with her family, who Van had relocated to Cambodia. They reached their destination in four days' time. Upon arrival, Tuyen was delighted to be reunited with her mother, Lo'an, and her siblings, who were very confused and afraid concerning the events of the past week. After explaining Van's position in the continuing Communist offensive and her love for him, Tuyen succeeded in calming everyone down.

Van devoted his energy to reestablishing contact with higher-ups in the Viet Cong hierarchy. Soon he realized that in the absence of Colonel Khan, there was a vast void of command within the Viet Cong. Van put out feelers to North Vietnamese commanders. He sensed that, given the vast losses that the Viet Cong had sustained, there was an immediate opportunity for the Communist North Vietnamese to infiltrate the command structure of the Viet Cong with their own people and make the Viet Cong a subsidiary to the North Vietnamese High Command. Van understood that in order to maintain his power base within the Viet Cong, he must consolidate what remained of the Viet Cong in the Mekong Delta and guarantee their allegiance to him.

After a week of gathering information, he concluded that only 50 percent of the Viet Cong in the Mekong Delta had survived the TET offensive. Van was also sure that since there had been no uprising of the local populace, the Allies could push the advantage they now had in terms of both economy and man power. The majority of the peasants would pledge allegiance to the Saigon government, and Van would be unable to replace his lost Viet Cong soldiers.

At Fort Hood, I spent my off hours studying the Vietnamese language and customs. None of my fellow soldiers paid any attention to what I was doing, as the majority of them had less than ninety days to serve. The exceptions to this situation were the young first and second lieutenants who were on their way to Vietnam and thought they knew everything. This created a volatile situation as the enlisted men were being put through riot control training prior to the Democratic Convention scheduled for August 1968. Since the majority of these men were going to be discharged prior to the Convention, they couldn't care less about riot control training.

I checked with my connection in Headquarters Company who was handling my reassignment to an intelligence unit in Saigon and was told that everything was in process, but, given the bureaucracy of the military establishment, I had to be patient. As a precaution, I had delivered only half the money to my contact, and I felt confident that I would be in Saigon within the next couple of months. I had cut off all contact with Jeri with great regret and kept only my father informed of my actions via phone.

Finally, on March 25, I received my orders assigning me to the Saigon intelligence unit. I was optimistic and excited about the future. I was acutely aware of the antiwar sentiment sweeping the United States and that there was a possibility of cancellation of United States troop support and economic funding. This, if it came to pass, would make my search for Tuyen very difficult.

I arrived after all at my new unit in Saigon in a positive and enthusiastic mood. I was only one of numerous intelligence clerks in the Saigon office of MACV Headquarters, and because of my prior experience in My Tho, it was obvious that I was an experienced and reliable intelligence clerk. My knowledge of the Vietnamese language and culture combined with my combat experience ensured that I was trusted with the highest priority intelligence reports. I was resented by my fellow clerks of lesser experience but respected because of my experience.

CHAPTER

25

Tuyen and Van settled into the routine of day-to-day life in their Cambodian sanctuary. Van was consumed with rebuilding the Viet Cong infrastructure and recruiting new members. Tuyen was content with reuniting with her family and spent her evenings with Van. She was concerned with how consumed Van was with the Communist cause and quickly realized that even when they were together, his soul was somewhere else. Having waited many years to spend the rest of her life with Van, Tuyen could only hope that as time went on, he would devote more of himself to their relationship.

It was a good time to be with her family and reconnect. Her mother was not one to become involved in political causes, only wanting her family to have a peaceful and happy existence. Since her husband's death, Lo'an had been a shell of her former self.

Seeing Tuyen's strong commitment to the Communist cause and Van, all that Lo'an hoped for was that their relationship overcome Van's singular focus. Having been uprooted from her native village for the first time in her life, Lo'an was adjusting to the realities of life in Cambodia. She devoted herself to stabilizing her family and reestablishing her relationship with Tuyen, who she felt was in need of guidance and direction.

They spoke of Van's commitment to Communism, his belief in celibacy, his violent outbursts, and his devotion to Tuyen. Lo'an felt that Van's priority was the Communist revolution, with his belief in celibacy connected therein. His violence was obviously a function of his demand for total loyalty. Van's love for Tuyen went unquestioned, but it appeared that this emotion was at the bottom of his list.

Then Tuyen revealed to her mother her physical and emotional relationship with me. Tuyen explained that her original intent was to obey the dictates of her Communist leadership and only obtain important intelligence information from me. She had been willing to use all of her feminine attributes in pursuit of this goal. She told her mother of Van's attempt to assassinate me in the restaurant and of the fact that had Tuyen not intervened, Van would have killed me during their escape. In relating these facts to Lo'an, she realized that her relationship with me had progressed beyond a source of information into a relationship based on consuming endearment.

She also told her mother that when Van had killed Colonel Khan and was about to kill me, she went into a state of shock and now realized that her actions were based on pure emotion. She now realized that on the trip to Cambodia, all she was able to think about was how ashamed she was at having misrepresented herself to me. She had used my emotional and physical dependence on her to achieve the goals of the Communist party. Her mother refrained from making any comments, as this was all too much for her to absorb.

I immersed myself in my new duties in Saigon and concentrated on ingratiating myself to my superiors through my experience and mature attitude. The Saigon post was no different from My Tho except in size. All of my cohorts went out every evening to enjoy the bar girls and indulge in drugs and booze. I had more important things on my mind—namely, how could I go about finding Tuyen? After a month of routine intelligence work, I became aware of a group within the office who dealt only with intelligence coming out of Cambodia. I set about doing everything I could to make myself invaluable to them and paid close attention as to when an opening might become available in the unit.

I socialized with the clerks as much as possible and displayed my knowledge of Cambodia and my experiences there. I was successful in attracting the attention of the highest-ranking enlisted man in the unit, and he assured me that within the month, he would pull some strings to have me transferred. I was ecstatic and worked even harder, spending my down time in my studies of the Vietnamese language and culture and trying not to despair the loss of Tuyen.

Finally, in the middle of May 1968, I was reassigned to the intelligence unit that handled Cambodia. I devoted myself to impressing my new superiors and getting along with the other clerks. I was shocked by reports of the decimation of the Viet Cong as a fighting force and of reports from the United States of growing antiwar sentiment. There were also rumors of a withdrawal of funding support from the United States Senate. Fact number one caused me to wonder whether Tuyen had even survived the TET offensive, and the second made me more aware of the possibility of a reduction in the number of American troops in Vietnam, which in turn would reduce the amount of time I had to find her.

The war continued with the Allied forces taking advantage of their decimation of the Communist forces during the TET offensive. However, it was very apparent that the American press corps had succeeded in portraying the TET offensive as a victory for the Communists and thus a defeat for the Allies. On the battlefield, the Communists were unsuccessful in their offensive, absorbing horrendous losses, but as a psychological victory, TET was an immense success. The American public was shocked by the ability of the Communists to attack at will even after the tons of bombs that had been dropped on North and South Vietnam and the horrendous number of casualties absorbed by the Communists. Given these facts, the North Vietnamese became more confident that the American public's devotion to the war had been undermined and that sooner or later, they would withdraw.

As far as the American public's commitment to the war effort, it was like a permanently receding tide. John Wayne was dead. The information I was receiving out of Cambodia indicated that shipments of supplies and ammunition down the Ho Chi Minh trail had resumed after the TET offensive at previous or higher levels than before, which indicated to me that the Viet Cong were rearming and recruiting replacements for further combat operations. The assaults at Khe Sahn and Dak To had ceased, and the countryside was relatively devoid of combat.

The South Vietnamese Government was continuing with its pacification program with what it felt were positive results. The Phoenix Program was instituted by the CIA under the direction of George Bush. This program revolved around assassination squads of Americans and Vietnamese tasked with killing leaders of the Viet Cong insurgency throughout Vietnam. From what I could surmise, the program was very effective in eliminating scores of Vietnamese based only on being pinpointed by South Vietnamese informants. In short, people were being killed based on the prejudices and personal vindictiveness of informants.

When I discussed this program with other clerks, I got the sense that these methods were part and parcel of any war and that I should turn a deaf ear and a blind eye to the actions. Checking further, I discovered that the Phoenix program had been patterned after covert operations used during World War II in Europe by the underground resistance fighters. Since the local populace was well aware of collaborators in their midst, the underground was quite successful in targeting local Nazi bureaucrats and their families. It was a nasty business with assassinations commonplace, as the underground forces had neither the freedom of movement nor the ability to enforce inquisitors' programs.

The advantage the underground had in Europe was that since the Nazis were the occupiers of many countries, it was obvious who the collaborators were. In Vietnam, things were different. Since the Americans were the occupiers, they had to depend on their Vietnamese counterparts for identifying potential targets, and it was not uncommon for personal and political agendas to be fulfilled by local informants.

It didn't take long for me to realize that the Phoenix Program didn't differ greatly from the atrocities committed by the Viet Cong during the TET offensive.

After several weeks of further investigation, I became aware of Cong Son island off the coast of Vietnam. The island was a political prison in use since 1867 by various regimes for interrogations of suspected enemy agents. All forms of torture were used in an effort to extract information. The term 'Tiger cages'"tiger cages" had long been in use, as prisoners were normally caged like tigers and immersed in water up to their necks in an effort to break them physically and mentally.

Very few prisoners survived Cong Son island, and many Vietnamese of interest captured in the Phoenix Program ended up in tiger cages there. I realized from previous experience that rocking the boat would only get me in hot water and thus I concentrated on positioning myself in the best manner possible to further my search for Tuyen. The item of greatest interest to me was the fact that many operatives used in the Phoenix Program and subsequent interrogations were SOG members. I planned to use the next phase of my mission to align myself with members of SOG in an effort to extract information from captured Viet Cong in order to find Tuyen and her lover. Within a short time, I had maneuvered myself into a position where I only handled interrogation reports from Cong Son island and SOG operatives. I noticed that 60 per cent of the assassinated and imprisoned Viet Cong operatives were turned in by 20 percent of the informants.

This fact made it obvious to me that these informants were using the program to further their own agendas and become more powerful in the South Vietnamese Allied political structure. I concentrated on reports from dependable agents in the Mekong Delta and SOG reports. To my amazement, I recognized the name Patrick on several of the reports coming from the SOG teams in the Delta as a member of the SOG teams stationed at My Tho. I once had a working relationship with him. Eventually, I sent a message to Patrick that I was in the Saigon intelligence office and that if he was ever in the area, we should get together. To my surprise, I received a quick reply that Patrick would be in the area within the week and would contact me. I saw this as the opening I had been waiting for to open the next phase of my search for Tuyen.

CHAPTER

26

Van continued in his day-to-day rebuilding of the Viet Cong infrastructure from his base in Cambodia. He had no problem getting supplies and munitions down the Ho Chi Minh trail but was having difficulty recruiting new members to replace the Viet Cong lost during the TET offensive. Villagers had seen the power of the Allied forces and were increasingly siding with the Saigon government. They were also shocked by the atrocities performed by the Viet Cong and thus more and more villagers began to reject the propaganda of the Communists.

Van had resorted to threats against family members and entire villages in order to fill the ranks of the men he had lost, but this tactic failed to bring in the type of dedicated Communist Van was used to recruiting. As a result, it became increasingly difficult to maintain order and discipline in the ranks. Van again resorted to making examples of the recruits who were deemed most likely to rebel, having them publicly flogged and then executing them himself. Van felt that terror was the only way to maintain discipline in this situation. Fortunately, he had a core cadre of mainline Communists who provided the discipline necessary to maintain a formidable fighting force. Van's most important task was reconnecting with the hierarchy of the Viet Cong command in Saigon in the absence of Colonel Khan.

In the month after the TET offensive, it had become apparent to me that the North Vietnamese were in the process of taking control of the power structure of the Viet Cong since the immense casualties incurred during the TET offensive. The deceased Colonel Khan was referred to only occasionally as a heroic martyr for the Communist cause, and Van said nothing to dispel this notion. He didn't care who was in control of the military forces in South Vietnam, as long as there was a way to achieve his goals of liberation for his country and guarantee his future with Tuyen. Van found the North Vietnamese directives after TET somewhat disturbing, perceiving them as condescending and submissive to the Saigon regime.

This all changed in April 1968, when reports emerged that Walter Cronkite, a preeminent American broadcaster visiting South Vietnam, had reported that the war was lost and the United States should remove itself from Vietnam. The North Vietnamese now realized that they had achieved a great political victory through the TET offensive in that it had broken the back of pro-war opinion in the United States. As a result, plans were in the making for another offensive. The thinking of the Communist High Command was that if they were able to replicate the TET offensive in any way, shape, or form, this would further prove to the American people and Congress that no matter what the Allies did in South Vietnam, the Communists would not give up. Nor would it make any difference the number of casualties inflicted upon the Vietnamese by bombing and infantry assaults.

The reality was that, as any populace, the Vietnamese people wished to be free at any cost. Given the supplies and munitions necessary to launch such an attack, the next major need was replacements for the thousands lost during the TET offensive. Van was informed that he had been chosen to travel throughout South Vietnam to train other commanders in the methods he used to recruit replacements. As a result, he and Tuyen spent little time together in Cambodia before Van was absent again.

Tuyen, having established her family properly in Cambodia, found herself with time on her hands. She volunteered to treat the wounded in the underground hospitals of Cambodia and was soon in charge of twenty nurses and working fifteen-hour shifts. This filled her days and left her so exhausted at night that she could only fall into a deep sleep. The sounds of war were constantly heard in the distance, and many of the wounded died due to lack of professional care.

Tuyen became very close to several of the older nurses, who one day asked about her relationship with Van. She explained their long-term commitment and was surprised to discover that none of the nurses and few of the patients held Van in high regard. The nurses knew of Van's tactics in recruiting recalcitrant peasants to the cause, going beyond torture to assassinations as part of his recruiting tactics, and the wounded related stories of Van abusing patients who he knew were of some influence in their villages when they refused to recruit fellow villagers. The abuse extended to withdrawing needed medications and starving wounded who would not cooperate.

Tuyen initially did not believe the stories of these atrocities. She could only believe that Van was currently instructing others in the hows and whys of coercing innocent Vietnamese into joining the Communist forces. She could not understand how the sweet young man she loved could have another side to him so evil.

Reflecting on the assassinations Van perpetrated on Toy Son island, the subsequent elimination of Alpha Company, and the assassination attempt on me, she could only conclude that the Communist cause controlled Van's actions. Anyone who stood in the way, including herself, was subject to brutal reprisal. Alone and confused, Tuyen sought out Lo-an's advice, telling her everything she knew about Van's actions.

Her mother, having already heard rumors about Van's tactics, had come to her own conclusions. She felt that Van was basically a good man who had been consumed by the Communist movement. As a result, she felt he had become immune to the morality

155

of normal society and behaved in a manner that condoned any action in order to achieve success. This attitude left little room for emotion and resulted in his denial of his sexual being and little room for any feelings for Tuyen. Any admission of affection for Tuyen, sexually or emotionally, would cripple Van in the brutal actions he must take in order to achieve his goals. Lo'an advised Tuyen to bide her time, look for a possible escape route, and leave Van and Cambodia.

Tuyen felt gratified at her mother's confirmation of her own feelings toward Van but could only hope that this conflict would end soon and Van would abandon his addiction to violence and become the caring individual she knew was hiding inside him.

CHAPTER
27

I went about my daily routine, keeping a constant eye out for any sources who could help me in my search for Tuyen. I was somewhat between a rock and a hard place, as I couldn't afford to have any of my coworkers suspect what I was doing. To all outward appearances, I was a dedicated intelligence clerk who preferred serving my remaining enlistment in Vietnam rather than anywhere else. I continued to solidify my relationship with anyone who had knowledge of activity in Cambodia and maintained contact with Patrick, the only member of the SOG teams I was familiar with.

Reports from the Delta and Cambodia indicated a return to the booby trap sniper war conducted prior to TET. As more and more Chieu Hoi (Viet Cong turncoats) entered the program, the pacification program appeared to be working. The problem became determining who was in fact a real Chieu Hoi and who was a Viet Cong agent. Patrick revealed that he was heavily involved with the program of weeding out the phonies, but, only having combat experience, he was sometimes at a loss to determine who was telling the truth. He proposed to me that a group of these Chieu Hoi be sent to Saigon to be interrogated by me, as I had intelligence and combat experience. I welcomed this opportunity as a means to ask captured Viet Cong who was in charge of the Viet Cong operations in the Mekong Delta and Cambodia.

This program commenced at the beginning of May 1968. I was entrusted with interrogating any Chieu Hoi who indicated the wish to give up their allegiance to Communism and join the Allied forces. My first order of the day was to free these men of any type of shackles and reject any form of physical intimidation. It was obvious that they had been abused by their captors both physically and mentally in ways that were not apparent but were very effective. Whether they were ARVN or American, treating them as human beings immediately gained their trust. Their greatest fear was being sent to the tiger cages and tortured.

Slowly but surely, I gained their trust by providing them with above-average food, clothing, housing, and the ability to contact their families. Any communication of this type was actually a means to determine who really was concerned about family members and who was actually a Viet Cong spy making contact with their controllers. A few weeks of this kind of treatment reaped huge rewards in the form of intelligence information.

Next, I decided to separate the Chieu Hoi as one would separate puppies from their kin to make them dependent on me. In this manner, I was able to extract information and compare one man's story to another's. By combining this information with the letters they were sending to their families and observing how the prisoners interacted with each other, I determined that five of the Chieu Hoi were Viet Cong. One in particular appeared to be in charge of this clique. Four of the suspected spies were sent to the tiger cages. I retained the leader of the group, deprived him of sleep and food, and eventually broke him. He revealed that the men were sent on a mission to infiltrate the Chieu Hoi program in order to nullify it and eventually participate in the next offensive.

I saw this as my opportunity to find out who was in charge of the Viet Cong infrastructure in the south. He revealed that Van was the overall commander and was now in Cambodia, but the spy had never met him. I took this information to the Chieu Hoi I trusted, and they confirmed that Van was their commander, although none had met him. They had only heard of his actions against anyone suspected of betraying the cause. Over a period of days, I was able to piece together Van's history. To my amazement, I discovered that Van was born and raised on Toy Son island, that he was in charge of the ambush that had destroyed Alpha Company, that it was Van's camp in Cambodia that was destroyed when I participated in the SOG mission, and that Van's superior officer in the Viet Cong infrastructure was Colonel Khan, who had died a martyr for the cause in My Tho during the TET offensive.

I was shocked to discover that my life and Van's so closely paralleled each other and realized that Colonel Khan was the officer who Van had killed when I last saw Tuyen. When asked about any romantic interest that Van may have, no one had any information. It appeared that Van had dedicated his life to the cause and would die attempting to free his country from foreign oppression. I knew that this was true but also knew in my heart of hearts that Tuyen was Van's paramour.

As I learned more information about the Viet Cong political structure, I realized the extent of the damage the Viet Cong had sustained as a result of the TET offensive. They had obviously been severely weakened. I surmised that if only they could be attacked in their Cambodian sanctuaries, they could be eliminated as a fighting force. Of course, this would never happen. The political apparatus of the United States Government would not allow any attacks to occur in Cambodia.

Reconnaissance reports from the Ho Chi Minh trail made it obvious that the resupply of the Viet Cong was back to its highest levels, and there could be only one purpose for this: another large-scale offensive. I sent this information up the line to my superiors with no immediate response. Knowing better than to push against an immovable rock, I decided to meet with Patrick as soon as possible and share the intelligence I had uncovered with him. This meeting took place in Saigon in early May 1968.

Over beers, Patrick and I reviewed who we knew in SOG, and I felt like I could trust him. I detailed the information I had uncovered about the Viet Cong infrastructure in the Mekong Delta, the continuing recruitment of villagers into the Viet Cong ranks, the resupply of the Viet Cong forces in Cambodia with what looked like preparation for another offensive, and the identification of Van as the head of the Viet Cong forces in the Mekong Delta.

Patrick was aware of much of this information but was especially pleased with learning the identity of the head of the Viet Cong. Patrick agreed with my assessment that the buildup of troops and supplies in Cambodia had the intent of triggering another offensive. He also agreed that the only way to convince the higher-ups of this possibility was to have overwhelming evidence behind this theory.

In order to continue to gather this information and further my search for Tuyen, I proposed reopening an intelligence office in My Tho, where I could interrogate Chieu Hoi captives in an atmosphere similar to their normal environment. I felt I could make them lower their guard by removing their fear of ending up in tiger cages and thus extract as much intelligence as possible. Patrick agreed that this was an excellent idea and told me that he would propose this plan to his superiors as soon as possible. I was moving closer to my goal of reuniting with Tuyen.

Patrick proceeded to contact his superiors about the feasibility of establishing an intelligence office in My Tho in order to interrogate Chieu Hoi in their home area of operations, thereby gaining their confidence and allowing them family visits. He presented this as a way to facilitate their cooperation and dedication to the Allied cause. Patrick proposed my name to head up this operation, reporting to the area intelligence officer but for the most part conducting interrogations and eliciting information as I so desired. Patrick argued that with my knowledge of the Vietnamese language and intelligence, interrogation, and combat experience, I was the most qualified enlisted personnel to carry out the mission with the highest potential for success.

Within a short time, we received approval for the operation, and I was reassigned to My Tho by the end of April 1968. I found the city in the midst of rebuilding but with a pro-Allied attitude and an emphasis on the future. I occupied the old barracks and office complex and converted them into holding cells and inter-rogation rooms. I was determined to allow no physical abuse in this unit, relying instead on time-tested psychological procedures to extract information. I had returned to My Tho somewhat a con-quering hero, having left the area during TET as a defeated lover. Now, I had returned in an authoritative role and knew that I would be able to gain information about Tuyen from the local people who knew her when she was there.

The first group of Chieu Hoi were frightened, not knowing what to expect. They spent their first few days being examined and treated by the medics and fed nutritious meals. There was no attempt at interrogation. We brought their families into My Tho as a safety precaution and a means of gaining their trust. The families were treated well with particular attention being given to security, as the families were just as unsettled as the Chieu Hoi. After a week of relaxation and good food, I interrogated each Chieu Hoi sepa-rately. There was no need for an interpreter, as my linguistic skills in Vietnamese had increased to the point where I could carry on a normal conversation easily.

At the beginning of each interview, I established the facts of the Chieu Hoi's original birthplace and activities within the Viet Cong organization. This was compared with the fact sheet each had filled out upon going over to the Allied side. The thought process was that the Chieu Hoi were disoriented and afraid when entering the program, and if they were spies, there would be dis-crepancies in their stories. These basic facts were then reviewed by existing Chieu Hoi from the area from which the individual origi-nated and the facts confirmed. In this manner Viet Cong spies were rooted out, and about 10 percent of the candidates were sent to the tiger cages for special treatment.

After the second week, the real interrogation began. Everything these men told me confirmed my belief that another offensive was planned for late 1968 and that plans were in progress for further recruiting and resupply of the Viet Cong in Cambodia and con-tinued apace. With each interview, I learned more about Van and his background. I learned of his family history, his rebelliousness as a youth, his commitment to Vietnam's freedom from foreign

161

control, and his movement up the chain of command in the Viet Cong infrastructure. There were hints at his romantic interest but no confirming facts as to who that might be. I knew all too well where his interest lay.

After several weeks of interrogations, a female Chieu Hoi named Lam was brought in. I was very suspicious, as she had many discrepancies in her background, but I knew that if I was to establish Tuyen's whereabouts, this woman was probably my best source of information. As a means to this end, I didn't send Lam to the tiger cages as I would normally but continued my interrogation. I quickly learned that this woman was very knowledgeable about Van's activities in the past year. She indicated that he had coordinated all the ground forces used in the TET offensive and that he was currently traveling throughout South Vietnam recruiting forces for the next major offensive.

When asked about Van's romantic involvement, Lam specifically mentioned Tuyen and went on at length about her relationship with Van from their childhood on Th oi Son Island, her recruitment as a spy, and her escape to Cambodia with Van after the TET offensive. It became obvious that Lam had a great deal of respect for Van, which bordered on love, and a great deal of jealousy, if not hatred, toward Tuyen. I realized that I could use these emotions to obtain more information about Tuyen, but I also realized that her relationship with Van was much more intense than I had realized and that it was possible that her entire relationship with me has been a farce.

I continued my questioning of other Chieu Hoi, obtaining valuable information as the weeks passed. The extent of the Viet Cong infiltration of the local villages became apparent, and the total corruption of the Saigon regime pulsated through the Chieu Hoi reports. Upon realizing the total corruption of the Saigon regime, I became convinced that there was no hope of winning this conflict because the population had no faith in the current regime. Even if the Allies were victorious, the average Vietnamese knew that his lot in life would not improve, whereas the Communists offered nationalization of land rights and equal distribution of wealth. The knowledge that there was no hope of progress under the current regime gave way to the belief that the Communists provided hope for a better future for Vietnam, and people would do many brave things in the name of hope.

As I continued my interrogation of Lam, I became convinced that Van's overwhelming dedication to the Communist cause had made him a predator who would stop at nothing to achieve the aims of the party. It was as if once Van had felt the power of command and the thrill of blood lust, he could not escape the adrenalin rush of these acts. Van was no different than the followers of the IRA, Castro, Hitler, or Stalin in that he had come to use the movement to participate in the horrors of torture and murder. He was a destroyer of lives—and he enjoyed it.

This insight into Van's mentality gave me both relief and horror. I was relieved to know that Tuyen would eventually realize the monster Van had become, making their relationship all the more unlikely, but I found horror in the knowledge that Van would never willingly allow Tuyen to leave his control. This could only lead to disaster. I realized that Lam was the key to locating Tuyen and making contact with her. I planned to use Lam as a double agent, returning her to Cambodia.

CHAPTER

28

Van had spent the last month obeying only one instruction from the North Vietnamese High Command: recruit as many South Vietnamese as possible to the Communist cause to replace the thousands lost during TET. This was a difficult assignment, as there was great resentment among the local populace toward the Viet Cong as a result of the assassinations and torture that had occurred during TET.

Van succeeded in donning his nice-guy persona and convinced many of the righteousness of the Communist cause. He relied on the overwhelming need of the average Vietnamese to control their own destiny. Despite the methods used by the Viet Cong during and after TET to eliminate the intelligentsia of South Vietnamese society, the average farmer only knew that the current regime was corrupt and of no use to him or his family. The promise of equality for all was preferable to the corruption and evil of the current regime.

As Van traveled and recruited, there were always those who resisted his propaganda, and, rather than be perceived as the bad guy, he had a crew of intimidators follow him in his journey. These men used threats and intimidation as a means to recruit, and if this did not work, they resorted to kidnapping, torture, and murder.

Van would meet his recruitment goals at all costs. He had become the preeminent commander in the Mekong Delta area, and, given the death of Colonel Khan, had taken over the direction of the Viet Cong. The North Vietnamese had infiltrated their people into the south but had not replaced Colonel Khan, as they needed someone like Van who would exercise control but not demand rank.

During his recruiting journey, Van made numerous contacts with the North Vietnamese High Command and impressed them with his knowledge of military tactics and insight into the minds of the Allied forces. All of this insight had come from Tuyen. Through me, she had deciphered that the Allied military leadership believed that body count was the only true indication of victory, and gaining control of the Vietnamese mind-set and soul was of little consequence.

It was apparent to Van that the United States military viewed all Asians as an inferior race with no ability to govern themselves and no backbone. It also seemed to Van that the North Vietnamese held the South Vietnamese in low regard and only treated him with respect because of his military experience, his contacts in the south, and his resorting to torture and murder of his own countrymen with no apparent pangs of conscience.

At the end of June, a meeting of high-ranking North Vietnamese commanders and the remaining leaders of the Viet Cong took place at the Ho Chi Minh trail near Ban Me Tho. Van was pleased to report that his recruiting tactics had worked and that the new recruits were being trained in Cambodia. The North Vietnamese revealed that another TET-like offensive was planned for fall. It was thought that, given the effect of TET on American support of the war, another attack so soon after the first would only reinforce negative American public opinion against the war. As far as Van was concerned, the sooner the better.

The North Vietnamese were convinced that by the end of the year, the American forces would start to be withdrawn from

Vietnam and the corrupt South Vietnamese government would be left to fend for itself. In the meantime, it was imperative to keep the pressure on the Allied forces through small-unit harassment, booby traps, and snipers. This would allow time for the training of new recruits in Cambodia in both tactical maneuvers and the psychology of the Communists. Much effort would be devoted to the brainwashing of the new recruits, as these men had been forced into the ranks of the Viet Cong and did not have the same religious fervor for the cause as the soldiers who had died during TET. Once a man gave over his mind to the cause, there was no turning back. Van was impressed by the strict organization of the North Vietnamese and their complete adherence to Communist doctrine—a much more pure outlook than Colonel Khan had parroted and one that Van could easily obey.

It became apparent at this conclave that the North Vietnamese planned to take over complete control of the Viet Cong in the South, but also had a need for people such as Van who had connections and leadership capabilities. Van did not like this situation, but he knew that if he played along now, he would be in a favorable position after the war was over. At no time did he consider Tuyen's fate in these matters; all that counted to him was the Communist victory and his future position within the structure.

During these meetings, Van was instructed to pass on to the rest of the recruiters his methods of rounding up new recruits for the cause. His main dictate was that these recruiters could not be stopped by any moral considerations when recruiting the local populace for the cause. All normal feelings of guilt and compassion must be put aside and every effort focused on rounding up bodies and minds for the coming assault. In addition to this imperative, Van made it clear that anyone not attaining the numbers of recruits assigned would be subject to critical review and possible elimination. Perform or die.

CHAPTER
29

Tuyen occupied her days caring for her family. She enjoyed the calm days that gave her body and mind physical and spiritual healing. The physical part was easy, but the spiritual was more difficult. In the space of a few short years, she had developed from an innocent country girl into a sophisticated, world-wise spy who had known many men. She had been saturated with the mind control of Communism, and this quiet period was the first time in her adult life that she'd had a tranquil time to focus on what she had been through, these events' effect on her soul, and what the future held. Having seen how Van and his cadre had treated the local populace in order to attain the ends of Communism, Tuyen had begun to question the basics of Communism and her relationship with Van as she knew it.

If Democracy and the Saigon regime represented materialism, greed, and total control of the peasant class and Communism represented redistribution of land and wealth but used murder and torture to attain these ends, then it would seem that neither provided a viable system that would nurture the lives of the common man. It became increasingly apparent to Tuyen that all mind-sets that attempted to control the human spirit according to their system's dictates inherently restricted the freedom of the individual to attain happiness and tranquility while contributing to the common good. It did not appear to her that it was possible to have a political system geared toward the common good that was not tainted by the weaknesses of the men controlling the system. Human weaknesses such as greed, hatred, racism, and the need to control others each contributed to the fallacy of a perfect system.

Tuyen concluded that placing herself in a position of neutrality toward the political factions affecting her would make her life easier and longer. This was a complete reversal of the firebrand, confrontational attitude that had enveloped her pre-TET as a revolutionary and Van's lover. As much as her rejection of political protocols had affected her life, Tuyen's attitude toward Van had taken the form of watchful waiting. She now realized that her existence in Van's life was secondary to the revolution. She also could not accept the brutality of Van and the other true revolutionaries toward the everyday Vietnamese.

Her thoughts turned more and more to me and my obvious gentle and caring approach to life. My reaction to combat was one of horror and disillusionment that men could inflict such brutality on each other. This attitude adhered closely to Tuyen's outlook on life after she had realized the horror that was being imposed on normal people by the revolutionaries and the Allies. She viewed me as a kindred spirit who loved her and whom she could learn to love.

In long, heartfelt conversations with Lo'an, she bared her soul and sought guidance. Depending on her Buddhist philosophy, Lo'an offered comfort to Tuyen and told her that she must be guided by the light posts of love and caring for others in order for her life to be complete. Tuyen gradually ascended to a higher plain spiritually, but mentally, she was torn between her former life and the future. The only thing she knew for sure was that she must search further for the essence of her existence.

CHAPTER
30

I continued vetting numerous Chieu Hoi applicants and determined that about 10 percent were Viet Cong agents. They were sent to the tiger cages. The remainder were acclimated into the routine of Allied military life, and their families were well taken care of. A great deal of intelligence information was extracted from these men. After about a month, they were sent into the field with various units under the control of well-trained United States troops who kept a close eye on them. It would have been very easy for a Chieu Hoi to lead a patrol into an ambush and disappear. This was, however, unlikely, as their families were under the control of the South Vietnamese Army, and no one wanted to guess what might happen to the family of a Chieu Hoi who turned out to be a traitor.

I kept a close eye on Lam, treating her well and awaiting some indication that she was willing to be a double agent. The biggest and best problem about Lam was that she had no immediate family. On one hand, she had nothing to lose except her life if she was proven to be a Communist spy, but on the other hand, she was alone and quite capable of becoming a double agent at very little risk to else. I devoted a great deal of time to Lam in an effort to uncover her background and, by so doing, take control of her spirit.

Eventually I discovered that she at one time was a devoted wife and had been totally apolitical. Her husband had been a farmer in the Mekong Delta who was also apolitical and only wished to be left alone by both sides. One day, the Viet Cong came through the village and conscripted her husband, and Lam had not seen or heard of him in many months. She agreed to work for the Viet Cong in hopes of finding her husband but had been unsuccessful.

I found out as much as I could about her husband and promised to do what I could to find him. In the meantime, I slowly but surely convinced Lam that the Communist cause was unjust and that the Allies held the only hope for a peaceful, united Vietnam. Patrick and I agreed that we would indoctrinate one of our most trusted Chieu Hoi in the background of Lam's husband and bring him forth as having witnessed his death as a result of Viet Cong ineptness—an example of what happened to a Vietnamese peasant who refused to make himself a tool of the revolution.

When I presented this Chieu Hoi to Lam, she realized that what he was saying must be true, as he knew a great deal about her husband and was very informed about the area where they lived and the time line of her husband's recruitment. Lam was shocked by the news that her husband was dead, and she reacted by withdrawing into a comatose state. For a week, she did not eat or drink and was taken to the hospital to be fed intravenously. Patrick and I feared that she would die. She was our best means of infiltrating Van's Cambodian operation. After a week, Lam began to return to reality and started eating and drinking again. As Lam recovered, it was as though she had returned as the person we had envisioned: a double agent devoted to the Allied cause. Lam was as a child ready to be formed in her parents' image and beliefs.

After several weeks of recuperation, Lam became stronger and developed a great enthusiasm for her new role as a double agent. We instilled in her a great love for the Allied cause and emphasized the advantages of the Democratic way and the negatives of communism. We made much of Viet Cong atrocities and brought in people from her village to testify as to the means by which the Viet Cong had recruited new soldiers. By the end of the month, we both felt confident we could send her back into the hands of the Viet Cong and rely on her to report on their activities. Van, the linchpin of the Communist effort in the south, was a special target.

The only thing that concerned me was the total lack of any mention by Lam of her husband. It was as if once she had been convinced of her husband's demise, she had removed him from her consciousness and replaced his memory with belief in the Allied cause and a desire to defeat the Communists. We remained concerned that Lam's elimination of her husband's memory would at some time lead to a nervous breakdown but decided that the risk was well worth it.

Lam was indoctrinated into a story of her time as a Chieu Hoi attempting to convince the Americans of her rejection of Communism and belief in the Allied cause. Part of her deception involved incurring a serious case of malaria that almost killed her. Her slow recovery would mask her brainwashing.

Once she had regained her strength, she was given a period of time to become proficient at being a double agent and fed sufficient Allied secret information to make her return to Cambodia triumphant. Lam was instructed to report any plans concerning future Viet Cong offensives and to be especially observant concerning the command structure of the Viet Cong in Cambodia and their means of communication in the south. By the time Lam left My Tho, she felt confident that she could achieve her mission and severely weaken the Viet Cong command structure in Cambodia. She didn't know how she would be able to gain knowledge about the Viet Cong command structure in Cambodia, but in her heart, she was committed to their destruction.

Upon her return, she reported to her immediate superior, who informed Lam that since her departure, there had been a change in the command structure in Cambodia and she would be debriefed by Tuyen, a confidant of Van. Lam remembered this name from her indoctrination and realized that this was an immense stroke of luck, bringing her very close to the inner circle of the Viet Cong command structure in Cambodia. When she was introduced to Tuyen, Lam immediately realized that she was a person of great competence and great loneliness. Lam was convinced that she could use both qualities to her advantage.

Tuyen was pleased with her new duties as intelligence coordinator. At the start, the work had been very boring, mostly processing reports on enemy troop movements and supplies. She was pleased when Lam returned from the Chieu Hoi program and immediately realized that she had a dangerous job on her hands. She must be absolutely certain that Lam had not been turned by the Allies. To accomplish this, Tuyen took on Van's persona—cold, calculating, and unforgiving. She first verified Lam's background, being familiar with that area of the Mekong Delta. Tuyen discovered that Lam had several neighbors in the Cambodian camp and was able to verify the facts of her life, including her husband's joining the Viet Cong reluctantly.

Tuyen questioned several Viet Cong who had served with her husband and was shocked to discover that Van had had him executed because of his refusal to fight. She realized she must find out if Lam was aware of this. Tuyen began her interrogation of Lam in a casual manner, laying a groundwork for mutual respect and friendship. Tuyen revealed to Lam her activities as a spy for the Viet Cong in order to establish a commonality of experience. Lam realized what Tuyen was attempting to accomplish and was eager to establish their relationship as equals. After several days, Tuyen and Lam became almost like long lost sisters, comparing experiences and emotions.

Finally, on the third day, Tuyen delved into the whereabouts of Lam's husband and was initially met with a wall of silence. It was apparent that Lam could not discuss her husband's situation without completely trusting the person she was speaking with. Realizing the situation, Tuyen revealed a part of herself no one else was familiar with, going into specific detail about her relationship with Van and the difficulty of competing with the Communist cause for his love. Lam had idolized Van and could identify with Tuyen's position.

Having established this basis of communication, Tuyen probed further into the whereabouts of Lam's husband. Lam revealed that he was recruited by the Viet Cong against his will but had done as he was told in order to protect Lam. She explained that he was killed by the Allied forces three months later and that she had hated the Allied forces ever since. This was the reason she had joined the Viet Cong and volunteered to become a double agent. As soon as Lam revealed the details of her husband's death, she fell silent and Tuyen was satisfied with the information she had extracted.

Next, Tuyen began to question Lam about how she was vetted by her interrogators in My Tho. As Lam went into detail about how she had gained the trust of the Allied interrogators, she mentioned that their leader's name was Tom. In a casual manner, Tuyen inquired as to the techniques that were used, Tom's fluency in Vietnamese, and any information about his background he may have revealed. Lam replied that her interrogator was quite fluent in Vietnamese words, although his idiomatic use was poor. She continued to say that he had recently returned to Vietnam because he loved the people and culture and that he planned to stay for as long as it would take to form Vietnam into a Democratic society.

Tuyen abruptly ended the daily interview and retreated to her living quarters. She was like a zombie, shocked beyond belief at what she had just learned. Lam's interrogator had to be me, having returned to Vietnam as an intelligence clerk in My Tho. This could only mean that I had returned to find her. Tuyen didn't know if she should be filled with fear or joy. She spent the rest of the day in a confusion of emotions concerning me, Van, and her future.

That night, Tuyen dreamed of reuniting with me, marrying, and returning with me to the United States. Upon awakening, the remnants of this dream haunted her and made her physically ill. As a result, she canceled all appointments for the day. She realized my return was both her worst nightmare and her most welcome dream. She was ecstatic that I had survived and pleased that I was devoting my life to the future of Vietnam; she even saw me as an escape route from her relationship with Van. What disturbed her most was the conflict between her strong commitment to the Communist cause in Vietnam and my commitment to Democracy.

As the long day progressed, Tuyen realized that any conjecture on her part about a future with me was ridiculous for several reasons. Number one: she was committed to the use of Communism to free Vinam from foreign domination. Number two, She: she was totally in love with Van and dedicated to their future together. Number three: presuming a Communist victory, it was obvious that I would be eliminated or imprisoned when the Communists took over. Finally, she couldn't see how any contact could ever be made between us, given the current political and military situation in Vietam and Cambodia.

After a day of consolidating her emotions, Tuyen resumed her interrogation of Lam and vowed to distance herself from any information Lam could provide about me. It was now time to confirm that Lam had not been converted to a double agent by her interrogators. Tuyen pressed her about why the interrogators were convinced that Lam could be trusted to return to her Communist brethren and convince them of her strong dedication to the Communist cause and the revolution.

Lam indicated to Tuyen that she was able to exhibit a fiery hatred for the Communists, who were destroying the fabric of Vietnamese life and creating a future of slave labor for the masses. She explained that these themes became the fabric of her interrogation responses from which she did not deviate. This consistency, she maintained, proved to her interrogators that she was committed to the defeat of the Communist revolution and reassured them of her reliability as a double agent.

Lam also realized that I was vulnerable to her commitment to the Allied cause. She didn't realize that I was inserting my love for Tuyen into my interrogation of Lam, unconsciously viewing Lam as my reconstructed version of Tuyen as I desired her to be after disavowing Communism and the revolution.

As Lam spoke about her conversations with her interrogators, Tuyen realized that I must have viewed Lam as a sanitized, reconstructed version of what I wished Tuyen to be. Throughout the day, she could not stop thinking about her relationship with the Revolution, Van, and me. Slowly but surely, Tuyen had allowed herself to reexamine all of these relationships in a very disorganized, but definitive, manner. This process was something that she resisted at first, because any analysis of her core beliefs, whether personal or political, threatened the foundation of her soul. Over the course of several days, she realized that she could not resist this examination and that she must decide what she really believed in and where her heart was leading her.

CHAPTER
31

Van had spent all of his time re-forming the Viet Cong in the south into a viable fighting force. Through physical threats and psychological intimidation of the citizenry, he and his cadre had succeeded in filling in the ranks of the Viet Cong lost in the TET offensive. He was now confronted with a twofold problem. Of most significance was the positioning of North Vietnamese command structure into the ranks of the surviving Viet Cong. This posed two severe problems.

First, the natural attitude of the North Vietnamese toward the population of the South was that of a superior race. They held the population of the South in contempt. Since the North Vietnamese held all the cards as far as supply of munitions to the south, there had to be a subservient attitude toward their command structure and a cooperative mind-set had to be established with Van's North Vietnamese commanders. Since the months following the TET offensive consisted of recruiting South Vietnamese peasants to the ranks of the Viet Cong and Van had been successful in this endeavor, he had solidified his position with the North

Vietnamese High Command and had become the highest-ranking officer in the Viet Cong High Command in the southern provinces, comparable in rank to a Colonel in the Allied forces.

As a result of his position, Van had direct access to the North Vietnamese cadre being sent south to replace soldiers lost during the TET offensive. Van used his chameleon-like personality to ingratiate himself with the North Vietnamese infiltrators, granted them his respect for what had been accomplished in the North, and emphasized the necessity of their presence in the restructuring of the Viet Cong as a fighting force. Secondly, he spent a great deal of time emphasizing the difference in the way the war was fought in the South as opposed to the way things were done in the Central Highlands and the DMZ. Van accomplished this by gradually exposing the North Vietnamese recruits to small-unit patrols, the watery world of the Mekong Delta, and the harsh environment in which this war was being fought. Finally, the cadres had to be conditioned to the idea that they must put aside their traditional contempt for the South Vietnamese and view them as the ammunition needed to effect a successful firing of their weapons.

Van was successful in his retraining of the North Vietnamese cadre and made a point of having several of those who couldn't put aside their prejudices assassinated while on patrol, making it appear they were normal casualties of combat. The elimination of those who would stand in the way of Van's objectives was a fact of life. Since Van was Colonel Khan's right-hand man in the Mekong Delta for some period of time, he had already established a reputation with the North Vietnamese High Command and had been successful in commanding a large force during the TET offensive. Both Van and the North Vietnamese realized that they were in a marriage of convenience, cemented by their joint commitment to the ideals of Communism and the removal of foreign control of all of Vietnam.

In high-level meetings with the Communist High Command, Van became aware of the deterioration of American civilian support of the war, which resulted in the belief of all concerned that the longer the war continued, the higher the Allied casualty count and the more likely an American withdrawal. What was needed were sacrificial lambs among the Viet Cong willing to sacrifice their lives for the cause. Van had no problem placing these men on the altar of war.

As he traveled through his area of operations, Van entreated his minions to constantly harass the Allied troops, inflicting as many casualties as possible while risking few Communist troops. The intent of the Communist High Command was as much to inflict wounds on enemy troops as to kill them. The philosophy behind this revolved around the idea that a wounded infantryman returned home as living evidence that the war could not be won and that the United States must remove its support of the corrupt South Vietnamese government.

At the same time, preparations for a second TET-size offensive were being made, and the timing would depend on the amount of munitions that could be moved down the Ho Chi Minh trail and how soon the new recruits could be counted on as a major fighting force. Van again determined to use the coolie labor that had transported supplies and munitions from North Vietnam into Cambodia as the core of his suicide squads.

CHAPTER
32

Patrick and I were called upon to report on our progress with the Chieu Hoi program to the top brass at MACV. The Allied High Command was interested in the veracity of the information being obtained and the percentage of recidivism prevalent in the program. After reviewing the statistics available to us, we came to the conclusion that the majority of the information being obtained through the program had been trustworthy after vetting the implanted Viet Cong and that less than 10 percent of the Chieu H oi had deserted the program. When analyzed, these figures made sense since the program provided a better life for all participants, protection for their families, and a much higher chance for survival.

Upon presenting our findings to the High Command, we were told to take a three-day R&R in Saigon and report back after it was over. We both welcomed the respite from the pressures of day-to-day interrogation and the opportunity to rest and see old friends. We also took advantage of this time to review our operational procedures and discuss how the program might be improved. Over several drinks that first night, Patrick revealed to me that he was in love with a Vietnamese lady who was now living in Saigon and asked me to cover for him the last two days of our vacation so that he could visit her.

Astounded at this revelation, I decided to reveal my love for Tuyen. Through mutual trust, both of us were relieved to have common ground and someone in whom we could confide about our emotional commitments. Patrick had started the process of paperwork needed to marry his lover and arrange for her immigration to the United States. I was disappointed to discover the length of time necessary to accomplish this but realized that this was the least of my problems, given the fact that Tuyen was a Communist spy in love with Van.

Patrick listened patiently to my story of unrequited love and of my belief that Tuyen was a person whose fundamental goodness could not allow her to participate in the type of repressive policies employed by the Communists to achieve their objectives, nor could she continue in her love of Van once she faced the fact that he was no longer the man she fell in love with. Patrick sympathized with my position and pledged to aid me in any way possible in my attempt to reunite with Tuyen. Obviously the key to any such possibility was Lam's infiltration of the Communist operation in Cambodia and any contact she could make with Tuyen.

We bonded in our commitment to our Vietnamese lovers and found solace and support in each others difficulty. Patrick spent the next two days with his lover, and I concentrated on what it would take to turn Tuyen away from Communism and Van. The obvious conclusion was that I couldn't formulate a plan until I knew where she was and tested her outlook toward her beliefs, and me, after all that had happened. I was convinced that there was an emotional bond between us that transcended our political beliefs. I believed the fact that she could have allowed Van to kill me during TET but instead saved my life was proof of a foundation for a future relationship between us. Having seen her compassionate side while she worked at the hospital, I was convinced of her basic goodness and love of her fellow man.

Having witnessed the methods that Van had used to achieve the goals of the Communist cause, I realized that I must somehow lead Tuyen down a path that led to her condemnation of Van's actions, ranging from his torture and killing of the Hu'ng family, his attempted assassination of me, and the methods he continued to use to recruit the native population to the Communist cause. I finally realized that the most compelling facet of Van's personality that I could use to convince Tuyen was that Van was totally committed to the success of the revolution—at the expense of his relationship with her. All these thoughts gave me a great sense of confidence in the possibility of winning her love. But at the same time, I felt depressed when I thought of the obstacles that confronted me in even making initial contact with her. I fell back on my core belief that my life would be nothing without Tuyen and that our love was predestined.

Upon returning from our three-day R&R, Patrick and I were summoned to headquarters for a review of our program. To our shock, we were informed that the High Command was so impressed with our results that we would travel around South Vietnam training others in the program.

This directive pleased us from the point of view that we were proud of what we had accomplished, but we also realized that this order would remove us from our base of operation in My Tho. I knew that this situation would severely limit my ability to make contact with Tuyen. Fortunately, we arranged that one of us must remain in My Tho and manage the existing program we had established while the other travelled South Vietnam training others. We were given thirty days to organize the program into written form, and it was decided that Patrick would take the first tour of training for thirty days while I maintained the current program in My Tho.

CHAPTER
33

As the days passed, Lam slowly but surely gained Tuyen's trust. This happened for several reasons. First, Lam's training in My Tho had prepared her well for any interrogations by Tuyen. Second, Lam sincerely hated the Communists because of the death of her husband. Finally, Tuyen was very lonely and unsure of her position within the revolution and confused about her relationship with Van. Lam sensed her weakness and sympathized with Tuyen, as she had experienced pain through her husband's death. Also, as a woman, Lam had experienced the pain of being a second-class citizen within the structure of Vietnamese society.

There was no room for women's liberation in any Eastern society of the 1960s. This societal organization worked well in the normal day-to-day life devoid of war, but as the tremendous toll of the revolution lessened the roll of the dominant male in Vietnamese society through casualties and absence, women were required to take over male roles in day-to-day activities. In Tu yen's case, this included taking a role in the war effort.

Since this added responsibility didn't entail added respect or increase a woman's position within Vietnamese society, women like Tuyen and Lam gained no respect for what they accomplished, nor did they see any improvement in the future. Gradually, as Tuyen became more confident in Lam's commitment to the revolution, Tuyen shared her frustrations and emotional instability with Lam. She recounted how she and Van had met as teenagers and became engrossed in the revolution. Through Vans activities on Toy Son island, Tuyen became aware of the necessity of violence in pursuing the overthrow of the Allied forces and condoned it. By engaging in spy activities and involvement with Colonel Khan, she had committed herself to the cause and put aside her natural revulsion against violence. She explained how as Van moved up the ladder of the revolutionary forces, he had used increasingly violent activities to achieve his goals. The turning point, she explained, was when Van had attempted to assassinate me at the restaurant.

Tuyen had been torn by her love of Van, her repulsion of the senseless violence of the revolution, and her emotional attachment to me. Her knowledge of Van's continuing use of torture and assassination in achieving the ends of the revolution forced her to examine her core values and her relationship with me. Lam did as much as she could to help confuse Tuyen.

Van was summoned to a High Command meeting with the heads of the North Vietnamese Communists and his counterparts in South Vietnam. He was well prepared for this meeting, as his recruitment tactics in his area of operations had been highly successful, and his teaching of these tactics to other Viet Cong leaders had resulted in increased Viet Cong membership throughout the area. It was revealed that the plan was to engage the Allied forces in another TET-like offensive toward the end of 1968. The emphasis would be on an attack on Hue, as it continued to be the center of Catholicism, intellectual resistance to the revolution, and a symbol of the old regime. Supply and ammunition buildup had continued in Cambodia, delivered through the port of Sihanoukville, as the Ho Chi Minh trail had been heavily bombed and damaged and with the cooperation of the Cambodians. Supplies were at the same level or higher as at TET.

There would be attacks throughout the country, but with increased security around the major cities, the element of surprise would not be present as it was during the TET offensive. The intent of the attack was to show the American public that Communist forces were still well supplied and numerically strong. The hope was that this would further disintegrate American support of the war at home. Van was pleased with the plan but disappointed with his role in the battle, since the majority of the attack would occur in the Central Highlands and Hue. Van was assured his role was important in the overall battle plan, first in supplying men and munitions to the actual areas under attack and then in harassing attacks in and around Saigon and the Mekong Delta.

Van argued that the majority of the South Vietnamese population resided in Saigon and the Mekong Delta. He presented the idea that if the intent of another TET offensive was to make an impact on public opinion in the United States, then the only way to have an effect was to base their major offensives on the Saigon area and perhaps to a lesser degree on various major population centers. Van realized that he was placing himself in a position of vulnerability to the North Vietnamese but sincerely believed that the original battle plan was of little use. Over a period of several days, the North Vietnamese saw the sense of Van's approach but did not commit to it entirely. A final decision would be made by fall 1968.

Van finally returned to the Cambodian sanctuary to oversee the further training of new recruits and see that the stockpiling of additional supplies and ammunition was on schedule. Once he saw all was in order, he had time to reestablish his relationship with Tuyen and her family. As usual, after such a long absence, there was a period of re-acquaintance between Tuyen and Van, and the addition of Tu yen's family made this all the more difficult. The real hindrances to their relationship were Van's added responsibilities with the planning of the new offensive and Tuyen's knowledge of the atrocities Van had committed in the name of the revolution. She continually looked at Van trying to find the loving, caring youth she had fallen in love with, but she saw only that he had been destroyed by the demons of war.

Tuyen reported to Van on her examination of Lam as a possible dual agent with the Americans, but Van was too preoccupied with furthering his career and preparing for future battle to pay much attention to another woman in the camp. Tuyen and Lam were left to their own designs. Slowly but surely, Tuyen relaxed and revealed to Lam who was who in the Viet Cong hierarchy in Cambodia, with Van at the top.

Lam could see the huge amounts of supplies and ammunition being brought in from Sihanoukville, obviously in preparation for another major battle. It was difficult for her to pinpoint exactly where she was located in Cambodia, but she had a general idea. It was Tuyen's plan to introduce Lam to as many Viet Cong as possible to see how they reacted to her. She also kept her ears open for any negative reports about her past life.

After four weeks of interaction, all reports were favorable and Tuyen trusted Lam both idealistically and emotionally enough to send her back into the Mekong Delta as a peasant to spy for the Communists. She also confided in Lam that she was very disenchanted with Van and wished for any information on me that Lam could discover. Lam departed on her mission, confident she had won confidence and was well positioned to be a double agent for the intelligence team in My Tho.

CHAPTER
34

Patrick and I began organizing our Chieu Hoi program in written form. Since Patrick was the field arm of the team, his function was to input procedures through me so as to have a workable training program. Being the inside man in the operation, I had the job of absorbing all the procedures and creating a teachable program that could be implemented in the field. This plan would allow Patrick to spend one week with me in My Tho sharing my field experience, and he would be able to spend the remaining three weeks with his Vietnamese lover. I would cover for him in My Tho, allowing him to control the existing program and interface with Lam.

The program itself would be designed around first weeding out any double agents in the midst of the Chieu Hoi. This was accomplished through intense psychological examination of the participants and thorough scrutiny of them by means of inquiries throughout the local community. Those who appeared to be bogus were sent to the tiger cages. Inevitably, some innocents were mislabeled spies. This was acceptable to the program as a cost of doing business.

The next step was for the survivors to be mined for any intelligence information they had and then retrained to the operational procedures of the Allied forces. Invariably, once the Chieu Hoi were reinvented as Allied soldiers, they were used in locations they were familiar with and placed in units as scouts in the most dangerous positions. They had gained what they saw as a position of importance within the group they perceived to be the future winners of the conflict, but they would never be trusted by their fellow combatants and were targets of reprisal by the Viet Cong. The only positive thing they had accomplished was protection for their families.

I methodically put together the program so the average intelligence soldier would be able to take what had been established and apply the basics of the program to their local situation.en the wide range of personnel needed to implement the program throughout Vietnam, once Patrick began his training of personnel, he had no time left to aid me in my day-to-day duties overseeing things. This situation worked to my advantage in two ways.

First, the demands of interrogating, vetting, and placing qualified Chieu Hoi filled my workdays from dawn to dusk. Second, I was able to quietly make inquiries as to Van's activities and location. Slowly but surely, I was able to put together an accurate profile of who Van was and what his activities had been in the past. I was amazed to discover that Van began his career on Toy Son island at the time I had been patrolling there. It didn't take a genius to figure out that Van had been the sniper who'd killed many of my companions in 1967.

Another Chieu Hoi who had been part of the force that ambushed A Company informed me that Van had been in command of that operation. Finally, Van's role in Cambodia was revealed and I realized how our lives had been intertwined, Van winning some battles and me winning others. When our involvement with Tuyen was added into the mix, it was eerie how much our lives were commingled, and it was apparent that our paths were destined to cross again.

Lam also revealed what she knew about Tu yen's background, from her youth on Toy Son island and her involvement with Van and the Communist movement, her activities as a spy in My Tho, and her involvement with Colonel Khan through her subsequent escape to Cambodia with Van. This insight into Tuyen's past allowed me to forgive her involvement with Communism and Van, considering that Tuyen became a Communist agent and fell in love with Van at an impressionable age. This knowledge reinforced my belief that it was possible, even probable, that her belief in Van and Communism must have been shaken as she matured and saw the reality of these formidable entities. I realized that I must find a way to meet with Tuyen , convince her of my love, and convince her to reexamine the core of her beliefs.

The obvious problem was how to accomplish this meeting without both of us being killed. I continued to interrogate Lam as to the next major offensive planned by the Communists. She emphasized the fact that huge amounts of supplies and armaments were being brought in through the Port of Sihanoukville, Cambodia. The game plan was to have a repeat of TET 1968 sometime in February of 1969, after the TET holiday was over. The hope was that the Allies would lower their guard when there was no attack at TET. The major problems with this plan were the training of the newly recruited Viet Cong and keeping the plans secret.

I prepared a summary of what I had learned and a time line for the next major offensive and presented this information to Patrick upon his return. Since Patrick had the ear and confidence of important officers in the intelligence community, we decided to make the report more detailed and use language that officers would appreciate. That meant that the information would be presented in such a manner that it was inferred rather than reported as fact, thus enabling the reader to take on the information supplied and report it as his own findings.

We had discovered that intelligence information was accepted by the hierarchy more readily if provided by higher-ranking intelligence officers. In our method of information sharing, we were able to attract the attention of the proper high-ranking officials in the intelligence community, and a great deal of interest in our program was generated. It was revealed to us that confirming reports had been received from other sources in the Communist community, and preparations were made to thwart the aims of the Communists.

CHAPTER

35

Lam slowly made her way back to the Intelligence headquarters at My Tho, gathering any information possible along the way. I debriefed her over the course of several days, and she went into detail as to the preparations being made by Van and his cohorts for the coming offensive. She revealed to me that an intense effort was being made to redouble the efforts of the coolies bringing supplies and munitions down the Ho Chi Minh trail in order to be ready for a major offensive in the coming winter. Large numbers of North Vietnamese had been brought in as commanders and heavy recruitment by Van had filled the ranks of the Viet Cong to their pre-TET levels. Although not as professional as before and not as cohesive as they once were, the Communist High Command felt they would be a force to be reckoned with.

Lam then shared that she had been able to form a sisterly bond with Tuyen and that it appeared that Tuyen was becoming more and more disenchanted with the Communist cause and Van. Lam also said that she had revealed to Tuyen that I had been her interrogator when she became a Chieu Hoi and that Tuyen had responded in a positive manner and wished to know more about why I had returned to Vietnam. My heart sang at this information, and that evening, I thought of nothing else but how I could make contact with Tuyen, win her over to my side, and rescue her from Cambodia.

As it was apparent that Lam was my only means of making contact with her, I decided to take a huge risk and confide in Lam my total commitment to Tuyen and my firm belief that she would someday become my wife. Lam reacted to my statement not only with surprise but with apprehension because she knew that Tuyen could remain loyal to Van and the Communist cause and turn Lam in as a traitor. In the end, she realized that, given her situation as a turncoat, it didn't make much difference if she took one more risk. Lam agreed to help me in my mission, and we spent several days deciding how to best approach Tuyen. The biggest problem facing us was how to deal with Tu yen's family, for we knew that she would not leave them in Van's clutches, and even if she did, this would subject them to a slow, agonizing death at his hands. We decided that some excuse must be made to move her family from Cambodia back to their hometown in the Mekong Delta, and if Tuyen agreed to any escape from Cambodia, she must be the one to formulate the plan.

More detailed reports were made of the Communist preparations for the coming assault. It seemed clear that their intent was to attack the major cities of Saigon, Hue, and Da Nang as they had during TET '68. This would be done to emphasize to the American public at home that regardless of the casualties inflicted on the Communists by the Allied forces, they would never give up. The Communists were willing to sacrifice all their combat troops in order to be victorious.

The 101st Airborne and the First Air Cav were beefed up for a major incursion into the Parrots Peak area of Cambodia. In conjunction with units of the South Vietnamese Army, the 101st Airborne, the First Air Cav, and numerous units of the South Vietnamese Army implemented numerous forays into this region. This was the culmination of efforts at the Vietnamization of the war, and everyone was pleased at how the South Vietnamese stood up against the Communists.

The First Air Cav straddled the enemy trails leading southward from the Cambodian border toward Saigon. The Viet Cong and North Vietnamese Army made desperate attempts to reestablish their logistical nets in the area with the aim of repeating the attacks of TET '68. During late fall and early winter Nineteen Sixty Nineof 1969, the First Air Cav fought a series of battles along these trails as three separate North Vietnamese Army divisions attempted to gain positions closer to the capitol. Although the Communist attacks were equally as strong as they had been a year earlier, their plans were frustrated by the wide-ranging Air Cav surveillance and mobility. The First Air Cav covered one thousand square miles of enemy territory.

During these operations it became apparent that there had to be large stockpiles of supplies and munitions in Cambodia, and the only way to damage the Communist attack capability was to actually enter Cambodia and destroy these sanctuaries It was decided that the first step in this interdiction was to severely limit the amount of supplies being brought in through Sihanoukville.

King Norodom Sihanouk came into power in the mid-1950s. His was a hereditary title that had installed him on the throne after the end of World War II. In 1955, United States Secretary of State John Foster Dulles attempted to convince the King to join the South East Asia Treaty Organization (SEATO), which was formed the year before as an alliance of Australia, France, Britain , New Zealand, Pakistan, the Philippines, Thailand, and the United States to prevent the spread of Communism in Southeast Asia. The king kindly declined the offer, preferring to adopt a neutral stance in the conflict between his neighbors and the United States.

Starting in the early 1960s, the North Vietnamese, taking advantage of Cambodia's neutrality, proceeded to expand the Ho Chi Minh trail in order to funnel supplies, munitions, and men into South Vietnam. This initiative had expanded into sup-ply depots, training facilities, and hospitals by the late 1960s, and although the King was becoming increasingly anti-Communist, he allowed the North Vietnamese free reign. Finally, in 1970, Henry Kissinger, President Nixon's assistant for National Security affairs, convinced Nixon to remove King Norodom Sihanouk and close the port at Sihanoukville, thus limiting the flow of munitions and supplies coming in from the south. A secret bombing campaign in Cambodia was begun against the Communist logistical bases. Known as Operation Breakfast, this initiative forced the Communists to move deeper into Cambodia, causing United States bombs to drop deeper into the Cambodian countryside.

The North Vietnamese didn't expect an incursion of more than a mile or two, but the Allied forces moved ten miles into Cambodia, seizing over fifteen hundred individual weapons, two hundred crew served weapons, three hundred fifty thousand rounds of fifty-one caliber ammunition, one million six hundred thousand rounds of AK-47 ammunition, and four hundred thousand rounds of thirty caliber ammunition. The United States dropped three times more explosives on Cambodia between 1970 and 1973 than were dropped on Japan during World War II, totaling approximately five hundred and forty thousand tons. This was the world that Tuyen had survived.

When Lam returned to the sanctuary of Cambodia and Tuyen, Van had just returned from his recruiting mission. During her debriefing by both Van and Tuyen, it became obvious to Lam that Van became very withdrawn at the mention of her husband. Lam inquired as to whether Van knew her husband or the circumstances of his death. Van indicated that he was familiar with Lam's husband as a would-be commander but was not personally acquainted with him. Lam realized that there was deceit behind this and determined to look further into her husband's death. During the debriefing, it became apparent to Lam that Van was treating Tuyen as an underling—nothing more. This made her more confident in her intention to reveal my wish to rendezvous with Tuyen. Lam passed on only enough information to make Van aware that the Allied forces would be more prepared for any future Communist attack, and nothing was said about Cambodia.

During the days that followed, Lam and Tuyen had long discussions about where the revolution was heading and the consequences of victory. They both came to the conclusion that they would be second-class citizens in a future Communist world, and this didn't fulfill their desire for recognition in the new order.

Several times during the course of these discussions, Tuyen made inquiries as to my state of mind and well-being.

Lam responded that I was as well as could be expected but was very frustrated with how the Allied hierarchy was waging the war. She described as most disturbing to me the knowledge that the American public was disenchanted with the war and that it would only a matter of time before financial support would be withdrawn.

Tuyen concluded from this information that my focus was on the establishment of Vietnam as a free country, independent of China, the United States, and Communism, which she now realized was exactly what she had dreamed of.

Lam decided to reveal to Tuyen my wish to have a rendezvous to explain my feelings for her and convince her of the incompatibility of the actions of the Communists, and Van in particular, in achieving these goals.

Tuyen was very confused and retreated to the wisdom only her mother could give her. During several days of commiseration, her mother constantly repeated the refrain of following one's heart in search of true fulfillment. This opened up Tuyen's outlook to the possibility that I might embody all the qualities that she needed in a companion for life. She also came to believe that I held beliefs that would someday result in the liberation of the Vietnamese people. The only way to be sure that Tuyen's speculation about me could be examined was by arranging a meeting with me.

Tuyen and her mother decided that they must arrange a plan whereby they returned to their home village and made arrangements for the rendezvous. Tuyen approached Van and explained that her mother couldn't adjust to life in the Cambodian sanctuary and was slowly wasting away. It was apparent that if Tuyen could not return her mother to her native village, her life would end prematurely. Van, too preoccupied with preparations for the coming attack to pay much attention, gave the order allowing their return to their Mekong Delta town. She requested that Lam accompany them, but Van would not allow this. Lam didn't want to go anyway, being preoccupied with discovering the truth about her husband's death.

In early December 1968, Tuyen, Lo'an, and siblings began the journey home. Appearing to be itinerant peasants, they slowly journeyed through the Mekong Delta. Tuyen confided in Lam that she must get word to me that she would be home by the early part of January, and I should make arrangements to meet her there. Lam requested to return to My Tho in order to learn more about the Allied plans, but in reality to inform me about Tuyen's whereabouts. As she prepared to depart for My Tho, operations were commencing in the Parrots Peak region, and the Communists experienced many casualties. It had become apparent that the Allies were increasing their efforts to interdict the Ho Chi Minh trail and cut off supplies to the Communists. Increasingly, supplies and munitions were being brought in through the port of Sihanoukville, which lay to the south of the Cambodian refuge. Lam made her way to My Tho and immediately contacted me. I was overwhelmed with the thought that Tuyen had not only agreed to meet with me but also appeared to be wavering in her belief in Communism. She must now realize that Van was no longer the person she fell in love with.

I began planning for the most important rendezvous of my life. During Lam's absence, I interrogated a Chieu Hoi who was from the same village as Lam and was coerced into joining the Viet Cong forces at the same time as her husband. Because I knew that Lam's greatest wish was to discover the facts of her husband's death, I allowed her to interrogate the Chieu Hoi, ostensibly to vet him as to his sincerity in going over to the Allied cause but really to discover what he might know about her husband's demise. The Chieu Hoi revealed that he was with Lam's husband at all times up until his death and was impressed by her husband's desire for peace and his nonviolent nature. The Chieu Hoi revealed to Lam that her husband's lack of desire for combat infuriated Van to the point that Van made an example of him and personally tortured him to death as a means of controlling his new recruits. Lam felt a coldness she had never felt before and committed herself to revenge.

I continued my day-to-day interrogations and became increasingly aware of the continuing Communist buildup of men and materials in Cambodia in preparation for the coming offensive. As the First Air Cav continued operations designed to interdict the stream of supplies coming down the Ho Chi Minh trail, larger and larger shipments were being redirected through the port of Siha noukville, Cambodia, due to King Norodom Sihanouk's commitment to neutrality. This had allowed the Communists to make use of the Cambodian sanctuary, and, in early 1969, President Nixon, Henry Kissinger, and the CIA decided it was time to secretly start bombing the sanctuaries in Cambodia. This effort, in conjunction with the First Air Cav's efforts along the Ho Chi Minh trail, in effect diminished any effort by the Communists to stage a repeat of TET 1968. Although extensive attacks were initiated, because of Allied readiness and pressure on supply lines, the effect was nowhere near what had been anticipated.

Meanwhile I conferred with Patrick and revealed Tuyen's request to meet with me, and we arranged to have Patrick take over my duties in My Tho when the meeting was to take place. I decided to have Lam be my emissary to Tuyen, Lam being someone we both trusted, and sent her on a mission to coordinate the meeting. This allowed a great deal of time to ponder her husband's fate and the complete disregard Van had for human life in pursuit of a Communist victory. Lam decided that her only goal in life was to revenge her husband's death and remove Tuyen from Van's sphere of influence.

It took Tuyen and her family a month to journey from Cambodia to Toy Son. It was mid- January 1969, by the time they arrived. They had been delayed time and time again by Allied patrols suspicious of their movements but had been successful in convincing all that the reason for their journey was her mother's health and need to return to Toy Son. After resting for several days, Tuyen welcomed the arrival of Lam and the news that I was eager to see her. She arranged care for Lo'an and contemplated how best to accomplish the meeting, knowing that both she and I would be placing our lives at great risk if detected. The Communists would eliminate Tuyen as a spy, and I would be placing myself in suspicion as a collaborator if caught.

Tuyen decided to arrange a meeting in Can Tho in the Mekong Delta, where she had relatives and which was a relatively safe haven, being controlled by the Allies. Both of us could travel there within twenty-four hours and remain rather inconspicuous. Lam revealed to Tuyen that she had information that led her to believe that Van was directly responsible for her husband's death. Tuyen considered this and concluded that it was entirely possible that it was true. She decided to see if I could verify this information. If true, this would confirm that Van's sociopathic personality was totally incompatible with her humanistic philosophy.

After conferring with her mother about how she should approach her meeting with me, Tuyen prepared for the journey. Lo'an's advice was, as usual, very logical. Her mother advised Tuyen to follow her heart and be convinced of my true feelings toward her, but, more importantly, toward the Vietnamese people. If Tuyen was convinced of the intensity and truthfulness of these feelings, she must find a way to escape Van and the Communists to be with me.

Lam returned to My Tho and informed me that Tuyen had agreed to meet me in two days' time at the home of her mother's sister. I recruited Patrick to take over my duties in My Tho for several days and departed a day early to be sure all would be ready when Tuyen arrived. The culmination of all my desires over the last two years was coming to fruition. I arrived in Can Tho and conferred with several intelligence personnel, learning that heavy fighting had broken out along the Ho Chi Minh trail, and secret bombing of the Cambodian sanctuaries had begun per the direct order of President Nixon. I was gratified by these actions, as I believed that Patrick's and my intelligence information had contributed to this action. Anything that could be done to interfere with the movement of supplies and munitions to the Communists was a benefit to the Allied cause. I obtained housing in Can Tho, reconned the house where I was to meet Tuyen, and prayed.

CHAPTER

36

Tuyen traveled by night to the most important meeting of her life. Her mind was a maze of confusion, rooted in her past beliefs in Communism and her unrealistic love for Van. She decided she would approach me with an open mind, judging me by my statements and refraining from making any conclusions based on physical contact.

She arrived at dawn at her relatives' house a day early and rested the next twenty-four hours in order to be clear-headed upon my arrival. Arrangements had been made for the occupants to be out of the house for two days, which would give us enough time to determine what the future held.

I arrived just after breakfast. It was as if the sun had just risen for both of us. We couldn't get enough of each other, emotionally or physically, but Tuyen made it clear that we must refrain from physical intimacy in order to realistically appraise our emotions. We each went into detail as to what had happened in our lives since last seeing each other, with Tuyen being open about everything but making no mention of Van.

I explained my rejection of my previous love and ties to the Western way of life and proceeded to impress upon Tuyen my commitment to improving the lot of the Vietnamese people. Tuyen explained that she still believed that Communism was a better system for her people than Democracy, but could not condone how the North Vietnamese and Viet Cong had implemented these beliefs.

In order to fully understand each other's emotions, we agreed to spend the day in quiet discussion and contemplation so that we could adjust to being together again. This was a slow process but worthwhile as we attempted to assimilate who we were and who we wished to be. In the evening, Tuyen slowly revealed how disenchanted she had become with Van's actions in the name of Communism. She had finally realized that Van had become a monster who believed that the only way to further Communism was through violence, torture, and murder. If this was true, then Van was a person without conscience who viewed all members of the human race as targets to be consumed in the name of the cause. This was not the man she fell in love with.

Once she had expressed her feelings aloud, she broke down in tears of regret and sorrow. I consoled her as best I could but realized that she must rid herself of all her previous feelings for Van and become open to the love of another. It had been a long day, and we agreed to retire to separate rooms for a night of spiritual renewal.

Neither of us achieved this objective. As dawn arrived, we arose with new hope for a new day. After a light breakfast, we renewed our conversation. Tuyen stated her belief that if she were to try to escape Van's control, she and her family would be subject to elimination. I reassured her that I had ways to protect them through the intelligence agency, but this would entail leaving the country. Tuyen absolutely refused to abandon her country and its nationalistic movement.

Realizing that I must find another way if I was to become part of Tu yen's life in the future, I began my story of escape from My Tho and my return to the United States. I explained to her that all aspects of life in America were abhorrent to me and that all I could think of was her, whether she had survived and where she was. I told her more about my rejection of Jeri, and my family and that I had only confided in my father.

Then I brought up Tu yen's intentions of spying for the Communists and using me as a source of information. She saw that I was hurt by the deception she had employed during our previous relationship. I made it clear to her that I had entrusted my life to the idea that my future revolved around being with her.

Tuyen replied that everything she had done was done in the cause of freeing her country from the grip of imperialism and that as a young woman, the only thing she was sure of was that the philosophy of the South Vietnamese regime was anti peasant and anti freedom. Since the only apparent means to remove this ideology and promote Vietnamese nationalism was the Communist movement, she had devoted her life to the revolution through them. She made it clear that although she may have innocently provided Van with information which led to his assassination attempt on me, she was without knowledge of the plan and would have warned me about it had she known.

She went on to say that while she still supported the Vietnamese nationalist movement, she had become totally repulsed by the means it used to indoctrinate and use the peasant class. What was the point of expelling one dictator for another that was equally repulsive? Part and parcel of this attitude was the growing realization that Van had become a monster whom even she despised and of whom she was in fear of her life.

I listened with an open heart and rejoiced in her rejection of Communism and Van and embraced a future with her where all things were possible. Neither of us had reached the point of facing the fact that if we committed to each other, our troubles were only beginning. Given that she adamantly refused to leave the country or her family, a way must be found to escape Van and Communism, yet work within the system for the freedom of her country. I felt that this could be accomplished through various American aid organizations but had not a clue as to how to go about it. First, I had to verify that Tuyen, given assurance of escape from her current situation and her desire for a position where she could help her people, also had it within her to promise love and commitment to me.

In the early evening, during the course of dinner, we discussed our feelings for each other. I told her that I wouldn't have returned to Vietnam had I not committed my soul to our future. She broke down and, baring her soul, admitted that ever since she had stopped Van from killing me, she had known that the only way she would ever be happy would be with me. Given the knowledge that I had returned to the States, Tuyen had given up on ever seeing me again and was shocked and thrilled when Lam had informed her of my search for her. We dissolved into an orgy of spiritual and sexual reunion of silence that lasted well into the night, the only sound our cries of rapture.

The next morning, we realized that we had made a decision which in itself would change our lives forever. The rub now was how to accomplish our commitment and survive. We decided that the best thing for Tuyen to do was to remain in her hometown with her mother, using her mother's health as an excuse to remain. As all reports out of Cambodia indicated that the massive bombing had continued, there was no reason to return. I had twelve months left on my enlistment and was determined to find a way to openly unite with Tuyen long before that. We separated enveloped by a cloud of euphoria, each committed to a new life and future.

Tuyen confided in Lo'an what had happened. Her mother could see the glow in her eyes and the exuberance of her spirit. I returned to My Tho determined to find a way to accomplish our goals.

Lam remained in My Tho to find out more about the circumstances of her husband's death. She learned that her husband had made it quite clear to the recruiters that he was a pacifist and was made a target of indoctrination by the recruiters as a result. When it became apparent that he was unwilling to bear arms, Van had him caged in the village square without food or water for days on end and whipped on a daily basis. When he held to his beliefs, Van had him dragged out and personally strangled him in front of all the villagers. Another example had been made. Everyone knew that either you committed to the cause or Van would kill you. Lam was more committed than ever revenging her husband's death.

Meanwhile Van was experiencing the might of Allied fire-power. Initially, the incursions of the First Air Cav along the Ho Chi Minh trail had severely slowed the flow of supplies and munitions into Cambodia. Sihanoukville helped, but when Nixon's secret bombing of Cambodia commenced, Van's supply lines became longer and longer. As the second TET offensive commenced, Van found the Allied forces much better prepared. In spite of suffering as many casualties as TET '68, Van's army had little to show in the way of success. He was forced to retreat back to Cambodia with his tail between his legs and a sullied reputation. Upon his return, he found chaos as a result of the bombings and commenced to reorganize the operation in Cambodia.

Since Tuyen had returned to her village with Lo'an, Van found himself increasingly dependent on Lam for backup organization and support. She became indispensable to him as time went on, and Van found his life much easier to deal with since there was no emotional attachment to her. As Lam wormed her way into confidence, she had to control her emotions. She bided her time and plotted the best way to effect Van's demise.

Van instructed his minions to revert back to hit-and-run tactics, booby traps, and snipers, since it was becoming obvious that support for the war back in the United States was disappearing; sooner or later, the Allies would run out of ammunition. Van then concentrated on cementing his relationship and improving his status with the North Vietnamese. Since the demise of Colonel Khan, Van's immediate superiors were North Vietnamese, and he knew that he commanded at their pleasure. The failure of TET 2 did nothing to improve his stature with his immediate superiors, as all they cared about was success. Van realized that the first order of business was to regroup deep in Cambodia, stockpile more supplies and ammunition, and retrain his surviving forces.

The North Vietnamese were sending more replacement troops to replace the Viet Cong lost in previous operations, and these troops had to be indoctrinated in the hit-and-run tactics of jungle warfare, as opposed to the frontal assaults used in the Central

Highlands. This was a difficult, time-consuming process, but Van realized that in order to succeed in combat in the Mekong Delta, it was the only way. Not only must he retrain the troops being supplied to him, he must convince his superiors of the efficacy of this idea. His North Vietnamese commanders were not used to this way of thinking, but he was eventually able to convince them; with this accomplished, the cadre fell in line quickly.

As the secret bombing of Cambodia continued, Van was hard pressed to maintain the supply chain down the Ho Chi Minh trail and depended more and more on supplies being delivered out of Sihanoukville. Rebel forces in Cambodia continued in their effort to depose King Norodom Sihanouk and, given the neutrality of Cambodia, this allowed the Vietnamese to operate freely within the country.

Obviously, the bombing campaign of Richard Nixon was a hindrance, but Van was used to being harassed and continually moved his arms and munitions stockpiles deeper into Cambodia. During the weeks of reorganization, Lam was at his side, gaining his trust and waiting for an opportune time for her revenge. Van hardly thought of Tuyen, and when he did, it was only as a possession whose value as a spy had been used up.

CHAPTER
37

Upon returning to My Tho and relieving Patrick, I was surprised to learn that Lam had spent a lot of time with the Chieu Hoi from her town and interviewed him extensively. I learned that the Chieu Hoi had revealed to Lam that Van was the person who assassinated her husband. Since Lam had returned to Cambodia, I was sure she was on an assassination mission. Although I didn't condone this activity, I knew that if Lam was successful, the threat to my and Tuyen's future would be removed and a major commander of the Viet Cong in the Mekong Delta would be eliminated.

Confiding in Patrick, I detailed my rendezvous with Tuyen and explained to him that I must find a way to ensure my safety, marry Tuyen, and remain in Vietnam. Patrick told me that he had heard of instances where United States servicemen had been assigned to the Peace Corps while in the military, married their Vietnamese lovers, and remained in Vietnam in order to improve the lives of the peasants. I immediately saw this as an answer to my and Tuyen's problem and determined to find out how to accomplish this.

In the meantime, reports out of Cambodia confirmed the damage the constant bombardment had done to Cambodia's sanctuaries. No reports had come in from Lam, so I could only sit and wait to see what had transpired. Meanwhile, Tuyen had settled into a daily routine with her family, allowing her a great deal of time to contemplate her recent decisions. She was adamant about freeing herself from Van's influence and to reevaluating what the Communist philosophy could do to aid her country.

Tuyen knew that the current South Vietnamese regime was totally corrupt, controlled by Catholics who had no need to aid the Buddhist peasantry and promised no hope for the common man. She also knew that the implementation of Communism in South Vietnam promised very little in the way of future benefit to these people. In fact, past actions only promised enslavement by the Communist hierarchy, and any benefits accrued would be for those in charge, just as things were currently. Most importantly, she had finally given in to her love of me, realizing my innate goodness and trusting her future life to me.

In confiding all these feelings to Lo'an, Tuyen found a soul mate who agreed with her conclusions and trusted her instincts. They both began a rededication to finding solace in their Buddhist beliefs. Buddhism did not revolve around guilt, fear, and retribution as its basic tenets. It was based in the belief that all souls are one, love of all sensate beings is part and parcel of life, and reincarnation is not uncommon. A complete rejection of the material world was necessary, and fulfillment was found in aiding others and reducing one's outlook to one of mutual benefit. Buddhism was open to new scientific information and, as a result, was a changing, dynamic belief.

This outlook was perfect for Tuyen's reincarnation as a loving, caring member of society and allowed her to reject her former life as an active Communist spy whose every waking moment was aimed at the destruction of all Allied personnel and the victory of Communism in Asia.

Lo'an joined her in this commitment. They proceeded to try to apply as much devotion to everyday life as possible. Tuyen did not know how I would view her renewed devotion to Buddhism but felt that, for the first time in her life, she could live each moment in the joy of pure spirituality. She was confident that if I was the kind of person she believed I was, I would accept her beliefs and hopefully follow them as well. At all times, Tuyen was aware of Communist spies within the village who, without question, were reporting her every move to Van. She decided that by making her devotion to Buddhism apparent in her daily life, this practice would be passed on to Van and he would decide to release her from his grip. In her heart of hearts, Tuyen knew that her new beliefs would be impossible for Van to accept since Communism demanded that its followers devote themselves to its tenets without interference. Tuyen was willing to chance Van's displeasure, confident in the belief that I was her savior and would protect her from all evil.

As I performed my normal intelligence duties, two major problems held my attention. First, I needed to make contact with Lam and convince her that she was too valuable an asset as a spy for the Allied cause to inflict revenge on Van for the murder of her husband. Secondly, I had to make discreet inquiries as to the possibility of my assignment to the Peace Corps before my enlistment was up so as to be able to unite with Tuyen as soon as possible. The first problem was at odds with what I desired because I knew that if Lam was to eliminate Van, this would alleviate the fear of revenge Tuyen lived under. Although I knew that, in order for me and Tuyen to survive, it would be necessary to eliminate Van, I also knew that the more information that Lam could pass on from Cambodia about the Communist plans, the more American lives would be saved. I could only pray that Lam would reappear before her need for revenge asserted itself.

As there was a Peace Corps detachment stationed in My Tho, I resorted to my old means of infiltrating their midst: by finding when and where they socialized and becoming part of their clique. The Peace Corps was notoriously underfunded, making it easy for me to ingratiate myself with them by providing some of the luxury items they had been doing without. I befriended one of their senior members who had served around the world and expressed my wish that I had joined the Peace Corps rather than allow myself to be drafted. I was pleased to be informed that there was a way to assign my enlistment from the Army to the Peace Corps, but this was a lengthy process with a lot of red tape. I indicated that I was very interested in finding out more about this and was assured that the information would be forthcoming.

CHAPTER

38

Van was deeply disturbed by the direction his Communist masters were taking. It was apparent that their intent was to infiltrate the ranks of the Viet Cong with their people so as to gain control of the organization. It also appeared that, as the Government of King Norodom Sihanouk in Cambodia crumbled, the North Vietnamese were making a concerted effort at taking over Cambodia in addition to their own country, which seriously harmed the Viet Cong effort in South Vietnam and depleted Van's forces.

As he was continually shoring up his relations with North Vietnamese commanders, he was forced to take time away from his primary function, which was to prepare his cadre for intensified action against the Allied forces. He was in desperate need of intelligence information from Lam about the Allied plans when she arrived in late March 1969, full of intelligence information. She informed him that the Allies were done with their bombing and incursions into Cambodia, bowing to United Nations entreaties to spare more civilian casualties.

Van was ecstatic about this news and had an elaborate meal prepared for Lam and his most trusted aids. Lam was seated at the place of honor at Van's right when, halfway through the meal, she attacked Van with a dagger. She was only able to wound him before being restrained by his aids. She was immediately imprisoned and would have been killed that evening, but Van, although weak, ordered her spared in order to extract as much information from her as possible.

After ten days, Van had sufficiently healed to begin his interrogation. Lam had been held under extreme duress and, as a result, was starving and dehydrated. Van immediately began to slice slivers of skin from her body in front of the assembled cadre. It did not take long for Lam to begin her confession. She admitted to being a spy for the Allies, feeding false information to the Communists, and wanting Van dead as a result of his murder of her husband. She also revealed that she had been instrumental in reuniting me and Tuyen.

This so enraged Van that he cut her head off with his own machete. Only now did Van realize how much he loved and needed Tuyen, more from a want of control than anything else. He retreated into a melancholy stupor, not eating or drinking for ten days. At the end of this period, he emerged with a plan to exact revenge on Tuyen. He would have to wait until the current offensive was concluded, but, secure in the knowledge that his position in the hierarchy of the Communist command was etched in stone, he was sure it would happen. Van sent agents to spy on Tuyen.

In the meantime, Tuyen , having no knowledge of these events, departed Toy Son to rendezvous with me. She was full of her renewed Buddhist belief and wished to share its wonder with me. We met in the same location as before and, this time with no hesitation, returned to the Nirvana of sexual fulfillment we had once had in My Tho.

After hours of lovemaking and a sumptuous meal, she proceeded to tell me of her new commitment to Buddhism and her wish for me to be committed also. I welcomed this instruction, as I had always been enamored of Eastern religions but never had had the time to learn more. My previous training in Catholicism had never satisfied my need for truth, honesty, and love but had made me feel guilty and afraid. My first instruction by Tuyen about Buddhism had given me a sense of tranquility and patience I had never felt before. This pleased Tuyen, as her religious faith had become part of her inner being.

I revealed my plan to become an advisor to the Peace Corps in My Tho, serving as an intelligence person and interpreter. I explained to her that this would take some time and negotiations but, if successful, would allow me to bring Tuyen and her family to My Tho, where we could marry legally. If all went well, I figured to have less than a year left on my enlistment, and I could then remain in the Peace Corps or become involved with some other agency that provided assistance to the Vietnamese.

Tuyen was thrilled with this idea and hopeful for the future. In the back of both of our minds was the threatening figure of Van. We parted with new found hope for the future and our commitment to Buddhism.

Upon her return to Toy Son, Tuyen was informed Lam's murder at Van's hand and was filled with dread and foreboding. She immediately realized that Van knew that Lam was a spy for the Americans and must be aware of her reunification with me and rejection of Van and Communism. She knew that Van would stop at nothing to exact revenge on us and immediately sent word to me about what had occurred. Tuyen was now constantly worried that Van's spies could be behind every tree and rock and lived in constant fear for her family's safety.

I realized that Van had eliminated his best spy and was sure that he knew that all the intelligence he had received from Lam was suspect. Worse than that, Van must know that Tuyen had betrayed him and the cause and reunited with me. She and her family were in immediate danger.

I quickly contacted the head of the Peace Corps in My Tho and requested immediate sanctuary for Tuyen's family, as her mother was seriously ill and the family depended on Tuyen for sustenance. I revealed nothing else, hoping only to gain protection for Tuyen and her family while he looked for a way to keep them in My Tho permanently. The process would take some time.

Meanwhile, Tuyen noticed that the villagers in Toy Son suddenly wanted nothing to do with her family. She assumed this was because Van's spies had been asking questions. An informant told her that a rumor had been spread that she was a spy for the Americans, and, as Toy Son was pro Viet Cong, no one trusted her. She knew that she and her family must remove themselves from Toy Son as soon as possible. She sent word to me through a trusted friend, and I sent word back that they must make their way to My Tho immediately and that I would provide them with protection.

We packed up our meager belongings and, with a trusted friend, set out for My Tho, about ten hours away. Since we had decided to take a less-traveled route, we encountered few fellow travelers, which was both good and bad. We assumed that Van's spies were following us. About three-quarters into the journey, we stopped for much-needed food and water. Suddenly, rifle fire erupted from the jungle, and everyone took cover. Fortunately the local militia was nearby and drove off the attackers. Tuyen had a minor flesh wound to her arm, but Lo'an was more seriously wounded, having been hit in the upper chest. We put together a makeshift stretcher, and the militia provided protection until we arrived in My Tho.

I immediately took them to the hospital, where Lo'an was attended to and operated on and Tuyen was treated. Her mother remained in the hospital with assurances that she would recover, and I took Tuyen to accommodations within the Peace Corps compound. As we discussed the ambush, we realized that it was the work of Van. The attack on herself and her family turned Tuyen's heart to stone for him.

Tuyen worked as needed within the Peace Corps compound and, due to her linguistic skills, became a welcome addition to the office. In addition, she used her clerical skills and personality to ingratiate herself to the management team and soon had them agree to provide food and housing for herself and her mother. Paperwork was begun to allow her family sanctuary in the Peace Corps, since they were targets of terrorist activity and were at risk of assassination.

Meanwhile, I continued to work on convincing my commander of my need to be assigned to the Peace Corps. Soon after

Tuyen's arrival, I had a nervous breakdown at my desk. I collapsed in tears and convulsions and was hospitalized for observation. The doctors concluded that I was suffering from a severe case of Post-Traumatic Stress Disorder (PTSD) due to the stress of previous combat and should be removed from my position in intelligence as soon as possible. The doctors suggested that I be returned to the United States and treated there, but I again requested transfer to the Peace Corps as an advisor. Under the condition that I continued therapy until my tour expired, my commander agreed.

Patrick and I had already trained a replacement for me so that in a matter of one week, I reported to the Peace Corps as an advisor. This allowed me daily access to Tuyen, who was ecstatic over this development. For the first time in a long time, I was looking forward to the future. Lo'an had recuperated, and she developed a strong and loving relationship with me. I fit into the daily routine of the Peace Corps, and it became apparent to everyone that Tuyen and I had become lovers.

After a month of romancing her, I asked for Tuyen's hand in marriage, which she happily agreed to. We were married in a Buddhist ceremony and spent our honeymoon in rest and tranquility in My Tho.

After a week of bliss, we returned to the Peace Corps compound and resumed our work with the local Vietnamese. We were living a life of love and fulfillment, but the presence of Van always lurked in the background.

CHAPTER

39

Van was consumed with rage for Tuyen when he learned of her marriage to me. He had an attitude of possession rather than love, and he vowed his revenge. In the meantime, he had to deal with continuous Allied bombing of the Cambodian sanctuaries and the failure of TET '69. Van had regrouped his forces deep in the Cambodian countryside in areas immune from the incessant bombing. His North Vietnamese commanders were highly displeased with the results of the last offensive and put extreme pressure on him to improve the capabilities and morale of his troops.

The good news was that by the end of 1969, the Ninth Infantry Division Riverine force would be turned over to the South Vietnamese and the American troops would be returned to the United States. This was positive on two fronts. First, Van knew that that the ARVN would not be as aggressive as the Americans in handling the Riverine force in the Mekong Delta, and secondly, it was the first real proof of an impending American withdrawal.

Van continued training his troops in hit-and-run operations, booby traps, and sniping at the enemy.

Supplies and ammunition continued to come down the Ho Chi Minh trail. Van's biggest problem continued to be recruiting new personnel to the Communist cause. There were several reasons for this. First, the male population of the Mekong Delta had been drained of men from the age of sixteen to sixty, either by the South Vietnamese Army or by Van's recruitment tactics. Secondly, the native population was tired of war, much like the population of the United States. The difference was that the Vietnamese had nowhere to go, since Vietnam was their home. Finally, the supply of food to Van's troops was almost nonexistent, as the average farmer had only enough to feed his family. Therefore, it was critical that supplies continued to be funneled to Van's forces in Cambodia.

With the overthrow of King Norodom Sihanouk's regime by Lon Nol, the port of Sihanoukville was no longer available to receive supplies via ships, placing more pressure on the Ho Chi Minh trail. Eventually, the bombing of Cambodia ceased and Van was able to concentrate on training troops and infiltrating his men into the Mekong Delta.

He also kept spies working to discover Tuyen's and my whereabouts. Revenge was a constant partner. Being a realist, Van knew that Tuyen was lost to him forever, but he hoped her devotion to the Communist philosophy would overcome her disgust at the means by which that philosophy was enforced. He thought if he could have an hour with Tuyen, he could explain the necessity of atrocities committed in the name of the revolution in order to be victorious. Barring that, the elimination of Tuyen and her family was a given.

Tuyen and I became accustomed to the daily routine of life at the Peace Corps enclave. I served as an advisor and interpreter, and Tuyen as a clerk and nurse. As there were fewer and fewer casualties, Tuyen was asked to organize a school to teach basic English to young Vietnamese children. As time went on, she expanded the curriculum into mathematics and composition. She found this very rewarding and a far cry from her activities as a spy.

I continued to divide my time between the Peace Corps compound and my duties interrogating Chieu Hoi prisoners. This was very time consuming, as Patrick was gone much of the time north of Saigon training intelligence personnel in the art of interrogation and vetting these prisoners. I was still very much a part of the interrogation program and, as time went on, I realized I could learn a great deal about Van's activities in this manner.

I firmly believed that Van would make an attempt at reconciliation with Tuyen and, failing this, would move to eradicate us. Obviously, I was depending on a victory for the Allies over the Communists, and if it worked out that the Communists were victorious, then we would have to leave the country. I had not discussed this with Tuyen, but Van was constantly on both of our minds.

Meanwhile, in the A Shau Valley near the Ho Chi Minh trail, elements of the 101st Airborne and the First Infantry Division ARVN prepared to reopen Fire base Ripcord in early March 1970. This was a major attempt by the Allies to severely hinder the supply lines of the NVA down the Ho Chi Minh trail. Due to weather restrictions, the operation was delayed until April.

Firebase Ripcord was successfully occupied in April, and patrols commenced in early May. Large concentrations of NVA troops were located, and air strikes and artillery bombardment commenced. The firebase was mortared constantly during the month of May, and, in spite of the Allied bombardment, the NVA made many attempts to assault the perimeter with human wave attacks. Numerous helicopters were shot down, including a CH-47 supply chopper.

By early July, it had become apparent that the NVA forces were so numerically superior and suicidal that when the next human wave attack came, the base would fall. The Allied forces obviously did not wish to be mired in another Khe Sahn quagmire; therefore, the infantry forces at Firebase Ripcord were removed and inserted to the rear of the known NVA units in order to seize their munitions and supplies, a mission that was accomplished with some degree of success. Firebase Ripcord was officially abandoned by the end of July 1970.

Van kept closely informed about the developments at Firebase Ripcord. He knew that with the reduction in American troop strength, this was the first major military operation that the ARVN forces would control, and this would give a strong indication of the ARVN's ability to stand on its own two feet. Although none of his units were involved in the fighting, Van realized that if the Allies were successful at Firebase Ripcord, the flow of supplies down the Ho Chi Minh trail would be severely curtailed. This supply route was more critical now than ever since the takeover of Cambodia by Lon Nol and the closing of the port of Sihanoukville to Communist shipping.

When it became apparent that Firebase Ripcord was being abandoned, Van exulted in the Communist victory. Now the Communists were assured of a constant supply of men and materials from North Vietnam. The attempt to establish Firebase Ripcord was the last major offensive conducted by American troops, and its failure signified a major victory for the Communists. They became convinced that without the American support, both manpower and airpower, the ARVN were incapable of controlling South Vietnam and the takeover by the Communist forces was inevitable. Now it was apparent that Van's supply chain would be uninterrupted and that, as the remaining American troops were withdrawn, the ARVN would become more susceptible.

After the debacle at Firebase Ripcord, Van concentrated on training and supplying his new recruits. Since it was apparent to everyone that South Vietnam would be under Communist control eventually, recruiting new cadre had become easier. As the pressure decreased on Van, he had more time to think about Tuyen and what had gone wrong with their relationship. He had only recently become aware of Tuyen's marriage to me and had to face the fact that there was no hope for their relationship.

Van was determined that if he could not have Tuyen, no one would. He dispatched trusted cohort Tran to My Tho to confirm the situation. Tran had numerous contacts in My Tho. During his time in Cambodia, he had frequently observed Tuyen performing her duties but never been introduced to her. Tran had admired Tuyen's beauty and grace from afar and was aware of her relationship with Van. He only knew that Tuyen had returned to her native village of Thoi Son with her ill mother.

Tran was shocked to discover not only that Tuyen and her mother had moved to My Tho but that she had married an American soldier in a Buddhist ceremony and was living in the Peace Corps compound. Upon further investigation, Tran discovered that the American soldier had once been in the intelligence unit and was now assigned to the Peace Corps as an interpreter, Tuyen had begun a school to teach English to young Vietnamese children, and her mother and siblings had joined her in the compound.

This was all very strange to Tran, who could only hope that Tuyen had found the ultimate cover for her spying as the wife of an American intelligence soldier.

Tran reported back to Van all he had discovered, confirming what Van had heard through the grapevine. Van revealed to Tran that Tuyen had defected to the Allied side and that her marriage was real. Tran became as enraged as Van at this fact and begged Van's permission to eliminate Tuyen and me as soon as possible as enemies of the people. Van gave his permission but insisted that it must look like we were victims of random violence rather than specific targets. Van hoped to hide his failure to keep his Vietnamese lover from his North Vietnamese superiors.

CHAPTER

40

Tuyen fell into a daily routine at the Peace Corps compound, spending her mornings teaching English to young Vietnamese and her afternoons as an office clerk. Three times a week, she went to the farmers market in My Tho to buy fresh vegetables and fish. She and I became more immersed in the Buddhist way of life and looked forward to my discharge from the Army and entry into the Peace Corps.

One day while shopping, Tuyen noticed Tran and immediately recognized him as one of Van's associates. She quickly returned home and waited in fear for my arrival. When I arrived, she explained to me that she was being watched by an associate of Van's, which could only mean one thing: Van's revenge was in the offing.

We decided to enact our own counterspy operation by my accompanying her to the marketplace so she could identify Tran to me. Upon arriving at the marketplace, Tuyen immediately spotted Tran and identified him. I decided to approach Tran in casual conversation.

We exchanged pleasantries and proceeded to a local coffee shop. After a cup of coffee, I shocked Tran by telling him that I was the husband of Tuyen and that she at one time was a companion of Van's. Tran showed no surprise at this information and acted as if he had never heard of Van. I made it clear that anyone who attempted to harm Tuyen or myself would be immediately subject to American military reprisal. Tran pretended that he had no idea what I was talking about and politely left the table.

Tran returned to Cambodia and reported his observation of Tuyen, leaving out the fact that he had been discovered and threatened, as he did not wish to incur the wrath of Van. This information confirmed Van's suspicions, and he determined to wait patiently for his revenge, realizing that the South Vietnamese government would eventually fall to the Communists and he would be able to control the situation.

Van's biggest concern was maintaining his position as the leader of what remained of the Viet Cong in Cambodia and the Mekong Delta while convincing the North Vietnamese who had filled the ranks of his fallen comrades of his leadership qualities and his knowledge of combat tactics. Additionally, he needed to fend off attempts by the North Vietnamese High Command to replace him with one of their own. He knew that he was the only one who could control the Viet Cong forces and wage war in a manner sufficient to achieve victory in the Mekong Delta.

To solidify his position with the North Vietnamese High Command, Van made sure that anyone who showed signs of leadership potential was assigned to menial tasks. If anyone moved up the ladder too far, he considered them a threat and had them eliminated. In this manner, he was able to keep his star at the forefront of his superiors and strengthen his command position. Only the few who were totally subservient to him were allowed into his inner circle.

Tran was one of the few, but although he appeared to be one of Van's most subservient henchmen, he hid a superior intellect and a thirst for command. Within Van's closest and most trusted cadre, Tran had developed his own followers who wished to accompany him in his rise up the ladder of Communist control. Tran had also volunteered himself as a spy to the North Vietnamese commander in charge of the Mekong Delta to report on Van's actions. Tran saw Van's loss of Tuyen and his need for revenge as a weakness he could exploit and made sure his North Vietnamese contact knew of the situation.

Tran was instructed by his North Vietnamese Commanders to keep them informed of Van's activities and in the meantime reconnect with me so as to elicit some sort of retaliatory action.

Tran returned to My Tho, with Van's permission, and arranged to have lunch with me. Tran admitted that he had been sent by Van to spy on Tuyen in anticipation of some sort of retaliatory action against her. He convinced me that he was on our side, as he didn't condone Van's sadistic means of controlling the Viet Cong cadre and hoped to replace him some day.

We decided that Tran would inform Van that Tuyen wished to meet with him in order to explain what had happened and why. Tran's plan was that he would ambush Van on his way to the meeting and assassinate him. Tuyen had no knowledge of this plot, and I didn't wish to be part of it—but I also knew that until Van was eliminated, we would have no peace.

Tran returned to Cambodia and informed Van of Tu yen's wish to explain things, and Van readily agreed. The reality was that Tuyen knew nothing of these plans, and I was only aware that Tran planned to eliminate Van. Tran drew on his cadre of followers to accompany him in an ambush attempt on Van at Can Tho. Van's need to either convince Tuyen of his love or eliminate her made him careless.

Van may have been careless, but he was not stupid. He instructed a member of his personal guard who looked very much like him to enter the meeting area as planned. Immediately, gunfire erupted and the impersonator was killed. Tran did not bother to verify the identity of the dead person. Fully believing that Van had been eliminated, he rushed back to Cambodia to claim Van's throne. Upon arrival, Tran declared to the cadre that he did everything he could to save Van, but the ambush force was too large. There was great consternation in the Communist camp, and the men decided to report Van's death to the High Command to determine his replacement.

Before this could occur, Van arrived on the scene with his bodyguard and took charge of the situation. Tran and his followers were rounded up and Van beheaded all of Tran's cadre. He then flayed Tran with a whip and pinioned him to a red ant hill. Red ants were flesh eaters, and, although it took some time, Tran was dead within twenty-four hours. Van had again made it clear what would happen to those who betrayed him.

Upon verifying that all of Tran's followers has been eliminated, Van was more convinced than ever that there would always be spies among his cadre and realized that it was of utmost importance that he be ever vigilant against any plot to undermine his authority. His paranoia increased, and he became as Caesar looking for his assassin Brutus. This was all to my and Tu yen's advantage, as Van now had to spend all his time protecting his position within the Communist hierarchy.

Supplies and munitions had been moved inland to Krajie, Cambodia, which already had a sizable Vietnamese population. Many caves and tunnels honeycombed the area, making this a perfect place to stockpile munitions and train new personnel. Van disguised his frustration with Tuyen with sixteen-hour days devoted to brainwashing young Vietnamese in the ways of Communism and making sure the new recruits had loyalty to him. He built up a new corps of followers who placed loyalty to him above the Communist party; in this manner, he became confident in his ability to control his men. He made sure that the Communist hierarchy was aware of his success with new recruits, without revealing that their loyalty was primarily to him. He only wished he could depend on such loyalty from Tuyen.

CHAPTER
41

My enlistment was expiring. The Peace Corps was ready to welcome me with open arms, but my superiors insisted I return to the United States to be discharged and make my own way back to Vietnam. I feared that once I left the country, it would be impossible to return, given the reduction of American forces and travel restrictions placed on civilians wishing to travel to South Vietnam.

I decided to confront my superiors with the threat of revealing my activity with the SOG forces in Cambodia, knowing that many regulations were broken and that if my activity was discovered, many heads would roll. My threat was successful, and I was allowed to remain with the Peace Corps. My role was now reversed—being employed full-time by the Peace Corps and acting as an advisor to the team handling Chieu Hoi turncoats.

I used the value of my expertise in the interrogation of prisoners and quickly attained the position of advisor , wherein I could do as I pleased. Life would have been perfect except for my realization that sooner or later, the North Vietnamese would be victorious and Tu yen, her family, and I would have to flee for our lives. I began to search for a way for all of us to remain in Southeast Asia. I knew that Tuyen would never agree to live in the United States. My only hope was to make connections with agencies dealing with the refugee situation existing in Cambodia and Vietnam. I set my sights in that direction.

Meanwhile, Tuyen was always on the alert for any spies emanating from Van's lair in Cambodia. None had been sighted since Tran had disappeared, and soon word was received of Tran's attempt to assassinate Van. Understanding that this epitomized Van's reaction to anyone who opposed or disobeyed him, Tu yen shuddered in fear.

The North Vietnamese leaders were becoming increasingly confident in their victory as the United States forces withdrew. Their concerns about Van's leadership centered around growing unrest within his command and the knowledge that he had been abandoned by Tuyen in favor of an American serviceman. The Communists realized that Van's leadership had been undermined and came to the conclusion that he could not be expected to function as a motivator and leader if he could not be successful in his personal life.

The Communist High Command moved forward with plans to replace Van when an appropriate replacement could be found. They also realized that he was still a consummate recruiter in the Mekong Delta, the largest civilian population in Vietnam, and thus was a huge source of manpower. They knew that Van had his own spy network working within his cadre; therefore, all preparations regarding his overthrow must be made in secrecy.

Van continued his daily routine and prepared for the worst. After many weeks of review, he set his sights on a twenty-year-old native of Thoi Son Island who he believed he could mold in his own image. His name was Lon, and he burned with the same fire for revolution as Van. He took Lon under his wing and proceeded to delve into his motivation for being a Communist. The facts were that Lon's entire family had been wiped out by Allied forces in bombing raids, and his beliefs were based on revenge against the Americans. Lon had been instrumental in revealing Tran's betrayal of Van and had in fact been his main torturer.

Van was impressed by Lon's loyalty and ability to perform violent acts in the name of the revolution. Now he proceeded to indoctrinate Lon in his belief that in order to further the revolution, any method was condoned. Van came to the conclusion that Lon possessed the lack of morals necessary to be a merciless leader and the strength of character needed to further the Communist cause.

My involvement with the Chieu Hoi program occupied 40 percent of my time. Patrick and I had recruited a cadre of interrogators expert in weeding out the turncoats who had been inserted into the program to be spies for the Communists. It became increasingly apparent that these counterspies were as interested in the activities of me and Tuyen as anything the Allied forces were doing. It was a dead giveaway when it was discovered that these men had a direct link to Van, and, as a result, they were subjected to more intense interrogation. In leading the interrogations, I was playing a game of reverse psychology with the prisoners.

Simultaneously, Van was spending as much time playing the political survival game with his North Vietnamese superiors as he was in preparing his people for any coming offensive. Taking these facts into account, I was confident that Van had too many concerns with his survival to spend a great deal of time planning his revenge on Tuyen and me.

The remainder of my time was spent working with the Peace Corps giving aid to refugees of the war. I was able to spend all of my evenings with Tuyen, delving further into Buddhism and convincing her of the inevitability of a North Vietnamese take over. Tuyen insisted that if this event came to pass, we must devote our lives to aiding refugees in the camps. I was in agreement. I continued my work with the Chieu Hoi program and thereby continued to draw out information about Van's activities. Tuyen devoted herself to establishing a school within the Peace Corps compound—an activity that filled her with contentment.

During the evenings and weekends, Tuyen spent her time educating me in the ways of Buddhism. She found this rewarding and also revealing in that by exposing me to the concepts of Buddhism, she was also able to recover her own beliefs. For my part, I found in Buddhism a pathway to healing and rebirth. In Buddhism I found solace, hope, and a belief in the magnificence of the moment I had never known before. In addition, we both realized that Buddhism afforded us a spiritual link that joined us forever and cemented our marriage. My mind-set was now based on an oriental perspective, believing in the sanctity of all life forms, previous lives, and reincarnation. I had completely rejected my old persona of Midwestern farm boy with its adherence to traditional values and had embraced the philosophy of the Orient.

I had no contact with my family or old friends, devoting myself to my new life and beliefs and subjugating myself to the path Buddhism directed. This cemented my relationship with Tuyen and her family and led me further along a path toward peace and tranquility. Meditation became a focus of my daily life, and as I calmed my mind through this practice, I became totally devoted to the humane treatment of all people.

With this commitment in hand, I began to interact with Father Gildo Domedici, a Jesuit missionary working with refugees in Cambodia and Thailand. Father Domedici's work began in 1971 as both Cambodian and Vietnamese refugees flocked to the camps in Thailand. Gradually, on a month-to-month basis, Tuyen and I travelled to these camps to serve as translators and attempt to establish schools. I saw this connection as a future refuge for when Vietnam fell to the Communists but kept this idea from Tuyen, concentrating instead on the humanitarian aspects of our mission. Tuyen became increasingly involved with the refugee crisis and saw our role as building a foundation for future work.

Father Domedici was born in Assisi, Italy, in 1935. When he was ten, his father passed away and he was educated by the Jesuits. At the age of twenty-two, he became a priest and was immediately assigned to Vietnam as a missionary. He would go on to become the Bishop of Dalat in 1978 and divide his time between his duties in Dalat and the refugee camps of Thailand.

He had known for some time that the Communists would be successful in taking over all of Vietnam. He spent much of his time in the refugee camps, and as he became acquainted with Tuyen and me, he realized that our future would be in aiding the Vietnamese refugees in Cambodia once Saigon fell. He had no problem with my conversion to Buddhism. He only cared about the fact that we were devoted to the cause of peace and that Tuyen would be able to establish schools in the refugee camps.

By early 1971, Father Domedici had established a strong bond with us and saw us as great humanitarians. As the year progressed, Tuyen spent all of her time establishing schools in the refugee camp with the aid of books and supplies from the Peace Corps. I was spending most of my time on my Peace Corps duties and delegating the majority of my Army duties to replacement personnel in the Chieu Hoi program. Through Patrick, I retained a source of information as to Van's whereabouts and activities and came to the conclusion that he was totally preoccupied with maintaining his position in the Communist hierarchy and recruiting cadre.

As 1972 progressed, it was a continuing repeat of the defeat of ARVN troops by the NVA at Lam Son 719 in March. At the battle of Snuoll in May 1971, the ARVN were again defeated in an attempt to trap the NVA in Cambodia. There were continuing battles around Saigon, but it was becoming obvious that without the support of the United States military forces, and with the cutoff of military supplies, the ARVN were incapable of defending their country. Even the massive use of Agent Orange, which denuded 15 percent of the countryside, did not deter the NVA from their objective.

I viewed these events with growing alarm and began to make Tuyen aware of the dangers facing us. I made it clear that she must prepare herself and her family for the fact that we would become refugees in Thailand. Tuyen cried for her family and country.

CHAPTER
42

I began to spend more of my time with the JRS group in Thailand. The main commodity these camps had was refugees. Overwhelmed by the numbers, Father Domedici turned to me and used my organizational skills to organize the refugees, with the first order of business being shelter. Food and water were being provided through the Peace Corps and various other aid agencies, but the most urgent need was to prepare the camps for the monsoon season and provide a sanitary environment to prevent large scale epidemics. This could only be accomplished by setting up shower facilities, efficient removal of human waste, and elimination of airborne diseases through the efficient application of health programs. Father Domedici provided education in the Catholic religion, and I recruited Buddhist monks to instruct the vast majority of people in the religion.

As conditions improved in the camps, Tuyen became active in establishing basic schools for the young and advanced training for more advanced students. Of equal importance was the need for doctors and nurses. Twenty-five percent of the refugee population was under the age of fifteen and very susceptible to disease. Tu yen spent half her time establishing basic medical practices and teaching the refugees about hygiene and daily cleanliness.

The biggest obstacle to this program was the nature of life in the refugee camps. Normal wake up was 6:00 am., and refugees proceeded to get in line for breakfast. If the line moved quickly, the individual would have consumed this meal by 8:00 am. In order to be served lunch by noon, one had to immediately get in line right after breakfast, which left no time for anything else. The same held true for dinner. This left little time for health care or education. In addition, the food served was barely enough to sustain life, much less provide enough energy to improve one's life. In addition, sanitary conditions were perfect for the breeding of mosquitoes, which spread malaria. Since there were no malaria pills available, the only way to contain the spread of this disease was to minimize the breeding of the insects.

In addition to malaria, typhoid and dengue fever always loomed on the horizon. All these diseases weakened the human body and made it susceptible to other diseases. Dengue fever was the hardest to contain and eradicate. Its symptoms were body aches, high fever, vomiting, and diarrhea. An after effect was susceptibility to hepatitis C, an infection of the liver that remains forever. Dengue fever was spread through unsanitary living conditions and mosquitoes. The conditions in the refugee camps were ideal for its infestation and spread. Considering this, it was fairly rare in My Tho and quickly suppressed. As a result, Tuyen and I were unaware of its danger.

As Tu yen's work at the hospital diminished, she devoted more of her time to organizing her school. Eventually, she had over two hundred students studying a curriculum of Mathematics, History, and, most importantly, English. She also pushed the study of the classics. She had enlisted the aid of six Vietnamese teachers who spoke and read English, and everyone was impressed with the progress of their students. The hope was that they would be able to expand this program into the refugee camps once the sanitation, medical, and food situations were stabilized.

This was my area of responsibility. Requisitioning supplies from the Peace Corps in addition to enlisting the aid of the Jesuit Relief

Corps, I slowly organized the refugee camps into some semblance of order and proceeded to set up facilities and enough food to sustain people through the day. This was a slow process that taxed my American patience. In addition, I still maintained my contacts with the Chieu Hoi program. There was still a great deal of recruitment and training to be done within the program, and my desire to keep track of Van's activities was a personal quest. It was obvious to us that Van would never give up his lust for revenge against us, and the best way to monitor his activities was by extracting as much information as I could from the Chieu Hoi who'd been in close contact with Van.

Tuyen continued with her nursing and teaching activities at the Peace Corps compound, always on the alert for Van's agents. Eventually, she relaxed her guard and concentrated on her daily activities and caring for her mother, Lo'An, and her siblings.

Unbeknownst to us, Van had dispatched a three-person team of assassins to eliminate us—including Tu yen's family. The team consisted of two men and a woman named Fan, who was a nurse. Fan was able to infiltrate the hospital facility in her capacity as a nurse, and the two other terrorists found work as laborers within the compound. Over the course of several weeks, they were able to pinpoint where Tuyen , myself, and her family resided and learn our daily schedules.

On a Thursday afternoon, Tuyen and I received an emergency call from the Jesuit relief agency in Thailand concerning a sudden influx of Cambodian refugees who required food and shelter. We left immediately and gave aid and comfort to the new refugees. We returned four days later to discover, to our horror, that Tu yen's family had been slaughtered. After our departure, the terrorists broke in to the family compound and tied up Lo'An and her two sons. Finding Tuyen and I absent, the assassins spent two hours torturing Lo'An to discover our whereabouts.

Lo'An finally broke and revealed that we were in Thailand, giving aid to Cambodian refugees. Once they discovered this, the terrorists doused Lo'An and her family with gasoline and set them on fire. The assassins escaped without accomplishing their mission. They disappeared into the countryside of the Mekong Delta, not daring to report their failure to Van, and we returned from our mission of mercy to find her family slaughtered family's remains.

Being devout Buddhists, we cried our tears and prayed for the souls of our loved ones and for a safe journey into their next lives. With Patrick's help, I had teams sent out to find the assassins. This was accomplished within a week. Their orders were to confirm that the attack was directed by Van and also to obtain this information at any cost. This work was done, and the information was passed on to me.

Tuyen was consumed with guilt over the assassination of her family and the means used to accomplish it. She knew that it was because of her allegiance and marriage to me that Van had enacted this horrible deed. Tuyen kept her rage at bay by clinging to her Buddhist beliefs. She understood that seeking revenge against Van would make her as much an animal as he. She devoted her energy to forgiveness and prayer for the souls of her family, and, in accordance with her beliefs, the rehabilitation of Van.

Tuyen knew her family was in a better place and that she would be one with them someday. She and I had long conversations about forgiveness and determined that the best thing we could do was to rededicate ourselves to giving aid to the Cambodian and Vietnamese in the refugee camps and cleanse ourselves totally of any thoughts of revenge.

Tuyen embraced this attitude, as was her nature. I outwardly attempted forgiveness but inwardly seethed with rage at Van and his actions. I secretly began to plan my revenge, as this was my nature.

CHAPTER

43

Van had his forces trained and supplied, awaiting orders from the Communist leadership as to when a major attack would commence. He had trouble keeping the morale of his troops high, as they were restricted to guerilla tactics. The major battles were being waged near the DMZ and in the Central Highlands, and the Communists were consistently victorious. Now that the Americans had withdrawn, the flow of munitions and supplies down the Ho Chi Minh trail had increased tenfold. It was apparent that South Vietnam would fall in a matter of months and the Communists would be victorious.

As a result of mounting casualties in the battles waged north of Saigon, 25 percent of Van's cadre had been requisitioned to replace the dead and wounded, which frustrated him to no end, as he wished to be in the midst of battle. As a result, Van had plenty of time to decide what he would do about Tuyen and me. He knew of our exodus to the refugee camps of Thailand and that we were working for the Peace Corps. He also knew that Tuyen would never leave Southeast Asia, as her soul was there, and that I could never leave her.

It was a simple matter to have one of his best agents infiltrate the refugee camp and report in detail as to our activities and devise a plan to eliminate us. Van preferred to capture us and bring us to a horrible death through torture, but, given our location, this would not be possible. Given the stage at which the conflict was in South Vietnam, Van knew he must bide his time and await the supreme victory of the Communist forces over the imperialists. He was sure this would happen within the year.

The Communists had experienced repeated victories in northern South Vietnam and the Central Highlands, and as a result, thousands of refugees had fled into the refugee camps of Thailand. In addition to leading to a Communist victory, this situation made the refugee camps islands of mass confusion, adding to Van's ability to infiltrate them. Time and circumstance were on his side.

Tuyen and I continued our work in bringing organization and medical stability to the camps. In addition, I was working with the United Nations High Command of Refugees (UNHCR). In this capacity, I was organizing the refugees to be sent to various countries as part of the relief effort. Those who had arrived in the refugee camps first were the first to be sent to countries that were willing to accept them. The United States was predominant in its willingness to accept refugees, with Canada, England, and Sweden not far behind.

In the back of my mind was the idea that this would be our final escape valve should the war spread to Thailand. I knew that Tuyen was unwilling to leave Southeast Asia, but if all was lost, at least we had a means of escape.

In March 1974, Tuyen discovered that she was pregnant. With enormous joy, we faced the reality of the world around us. Because of the limited food and primitive medical facilities, I insisted that Tuyen restrict her activities so as to have a normal pregnancy. Tuyen did her best to take my advice, but with the need so great from the refugees, she found this difficult. I assigned her an aid to ease her workload. Aside from the usual morning sickness, all went well. My duties with the UNHCR took up more and more of my time as the receiving countries prepared for the refugees.

My duties entailed screening potential immigrants for disease and making sure that they were among the first to arrive in the camps. This was a time-consuming process, but very rewarding when I could see the joy on the faces of those who successfully left the camps. In addition, I still worked with the Peace Corps to acquire much-needed medical supplies and building materials. In this capacity, I was able to provide Tuyen with extra food supplies in order to guarantee the health of our child. To date, her pregnancy was normal with no contingent problems. The depression that had consumed her after her family's assassination had dissipated. In the joy of her pregnancy, she was able to block out the darkness of the conditions of the refugee camp and concentrate on having a healthy baby.

My duties with the UNHCR were expanding. My time was consumed by creating an infrastructure that would facilitate the movement of refugees to foreign countries when the time came. This entailed examinations for disease, job capabilities, and ultimately, areas where the refugees could be moved to with the promise of training and survival. Starting from ground zero, there was much work to be done.

I began, with the help of Tuyen, to establish cadre who were capable of screening applicants' health wise and determining their capabilities. This took a great deal of time, for once a refugee was approved for immigration, there was as yet nowhere for them to go. The problem was solved by using the initial approved applicants to screen incoming applicants, and by August of 1974, the first refugees were sent to training camps in the United States and Canada.

Tu yen's pregnancy continued as planned, and the baby was due in December. South Vietnam was increasingly under control of the Communists. Van, meanwhile, was preparing his forces for a major push into the Mekong Delta and Saigon. During the fall of 1974, his cadre continued to harass ARVN troops with sniper fire, booby traps, and small-unit ambushes. Van kept his troops' morale up by promising them that the final offensive would occur in the next six months and then, the Vietnamese would be in charge of their own destiny. He had been made aware of Tuyen's pregnancy through spies he had placed within the refugee camps and was also aware of my activities within the UNHCR. These facts further inflamed his desire to have revenge on us. He would only be satisfied by the ultimate revenge of our death and the death of our child.

His agent in Tuyen's camp gradually worked her way into Tuyen's confidence and became her maid. Her name was Li, and from her birth she had been a part of the Communist movement. Her parents and brothers were all active in Van's cadre, either as combatants or in the supply chain. She was well versed in being a midwife and was of great help to Tuyen. Through the numerous hours they spent together, the two women became fast friends. Although Li was not an assassin, she was well versed in information gathering and provided a constant stream of information to Van.

Van's instructions from his Communist masters were to continue the harassment of ARVN troops into early 1975, when all would be ready for an all-out offensive into the Mekong Delta and Saigon. The Communists had already taken over a great deal of the northern provinces of South Vietnam in late 1974, and as the United States had cut off munitions and supplies to the South Vietnamese forces, the Communists were confident of victory. The populace of South Vietnam was leaning toward the Communists, as they appeared to be the eventual victors in the conflict.

Tuyen and I prepared for the birth of our baby as 1974 drew to a close. We could only hope for the best, but I knew that in order for our child to be brought up properly, we must flee the refugee camp and South Vietnam before the Communists were victorious. At best this would be difficult for Tuyen.

Behind the scenes, I made preparations for us to flee. With my connections in the immigration of refugees to the United States, the way out was easy yet still difficult. Quotas had been set, and getting around these would be difficult given the enormity of the refugee population. Li aided Tuyen immensely as Tuyen suffered from morning sickness and poor nourishment, although her diet was significantly better than that of anyone else in the camp. Li also inserted herself into Tuyen's work life, as I had made a significant effort to limit Tuyen's physical expenditure.

The baby was due in one month's time, and I was concerned as to what the future held. The Communists had taken over most of the northern provinces of South Vietnam, and it was apparent that by spring, the entire country would fall. As the situation worsened, refugees poured into the camps in Thailand, straining an already overwhelmed system. I made arrangements through my superiors to make space available as soon as possible on refugee flights out of Saigon. This would be a difficult task given the number of people attempting to leave the camps, but it was always a matter of who you knew, not what you knew.

Van was moving his forces toward Saigon, still concentrating on guerilla tactics as he prepared for the takeover. He was constantly updated on Tuyen's status by Li but was unaware of my plans to flee the country, as was Tuyen. The baby was born in early January 1975, but everyone was horrified to discover that she had been born blind. The doctors attributed this to my exposure to Agent Orange, although Tuyen held herself responsible due to her depression over the loss of her family. Both of us were inconsolable.

The situation in South Vietnam and in the refugee camps continued to deteriorate. I realized the fall of the Saigon government was inevitable and knew that the most dependable way to get my family out of Vietnam was to resort to the time-honored method of bribery. Through contacts I had with the South Vietnamese government, I pursued this path. Van, meanwhile, exulted in the news that our baby has been born blind. He assumed this was a judgment from the gods against Tuyen for marrying an American. He continued to receive reports from Li as to Tuyen's activities.

As 1975 evolved, Communist troops came to control three-quarters of the country. Van's forces rolled toward Saigon using tried and true large-unit combat tactics. I discovered that abandoned babies were being flown out of Saigon, and, with the payment of a large cash bribe, I arranged for our child to be on one of the first flights out. When I proposed my plan to Tuyen, she protested vigorously but eventually realized that this was best for all concerned.

Unfortunately, she revealed the escape plan to Li, who immediately informed Van. Through his sources in the South Vietnamese government, Van discovered the flight number the baby would be taking. Through the payment of a large bribe, Van had a baggage handler hide a bomb on board the flight.

Tuyen and I accompanied the baby to the airport, and tearfully watched the plane take off. We were horrified to hear that the flight exploded in midair shortly after takeoff and that there were no survivors. Van was ecstatic; he had his revenge.

CHAPTER

44

We retreated in a state of total emotional and physical collapse to the chaos of the refugee camp. The dangerous weeklong journey had kept our minds occupied, clouding the reality of the tragedy that had befallen us. Once amongst our fellow Peace Corps workers, we were treated with gentle love, both physically and emotionally. The ministrations of our fellow caregivers were appreciated, but did little to lessen our misery.

Tuyen remained secluded in the sorrowful fog engendered by this tragedy while I was at least able to occupy my day in the duties of my job. Both of us constantly questioned why these tragedies had befallen our family, but the answer escaped us. Li was in as much pain as we were, knowing that the information she had given Van about the baby's departure had led to the plane exploding and our baby's death, as well as the deaths of numerous other babies. Tuyen and I had no desire to know what had caused the plane to crash.

Several months passed during which Tuyen began to waste away to nothing as a result of her despair. Li was horrified to hear that Van was reveling in the death of this innocent child and bragging that it was his victory.

In the meantime, Communist forces had overrun Saigon, and any South Vietnamese who had aided the Allies did everything they could to escape from the Communists. The Saigon government fell in April 1975, and the streets of Saigon were jammed with exuberant Communists. What had started as a rag-tag rebellion had defeated the most powerful nation on earth and its Allies.

Van rejoiced also, looking to the future with no regret for the thousands of lives lost, the hundreds tortured to death, or the relationships destroyed. Victory made every act committed an act of independence. He felt sad that the fighting was over, as that was all he had known since childhood, and he felt personally depressed and contemptuous toward the victorious North Vietnamese. Van saw himself as a revolutionary nationalist, not as a bureaucratic Communist. The focus of his life had been the expulsion of foreign nations from Vietnamese soil, and this had been accomplished.

What remained to be seen now was how the North Vietnamese implemented their brand of Communism in South Vietnam. As a result of his exposure to North Vietnamese philosophy after the removal of Colonel Khan, Van had much to be concerned about. First and foremost, he knew that the North Vietnamese had a negative attitude toward the South Vietnamese for the first few months of the North Vietnamese takeover of South Vietnam, and chaos was a way of life in South Vietnam.

Allied sympathizers were still trying to escape and if they resisted, they were shot. After two months, the North Vietnamese High Command decided that all South Vietnamese sympathizers with the Allies were to be sent to reeducation camps within South Vietnam. The task of establishing these camps and deciding how the reeducation was to be accomplished was assigned to Van as a result of his success in recruiting unwilling South Vietnamese to be Viet Cong cadre. The easiest way to accomplish this was through the use of informants. Members of the Army of the Republic of South Vietnam (ARVN) were easily rounded up. Civilian sympathizers for the Allied cause were harder to root out. Neighbor turned against neighbor, and in many cases, it was a matter of who got to the investigators first. As a result, many Vietnamese who had not been involved with either side were rounded up. Van only cared about the numbers.

The original plan was to reeducate these captives over a period of one year. Classes held for five hours in the morning consisted of anti-American brainwashing and Communist theory. Afternoons were spent in physical labor in the fields. Food was never plentiful, sanitation was nonexistent, and disease ravaged the camps. Van's goal was a 50 percent survival rate—the fewer survivors, the fewer mouths to feed. Those who made it through the year of reeducation could be seen as candidates for release to the general population.

Very few were actually released, as the reorganization of South Vietnamese society proceeded slowly. The exodus of two million freedom-loving South Vietnamese to refugee camps in Thailand and boat-people was a favor to the Communists. Within the reeducation camps, intellectuals and members of any religious clergy were rooted out and eliminated. Religion was viewed as the opium of the masses, and Van realized that he had a talent for this type of mission. His ultimate goal remained the elimination of Tuyen and me.

CHAPTER
45

Tuyen and I continued going through the motions of living. Neither one of us could see beyond each day, so engulfed were we by the tragedy that had befallen us. Childless again, our emotional core had been destroyed by Van's murder of our baby.

"I hope Van finds us and eliminates us," Tuyen said over and over.

I agreed, but deep down in the depths of my soul, I had a deep-seated need to torture Van and then kill him.

As space was filled, refugees camped outside with no food, no shelter, contaminated water, and rampant disease. Fate was eliminating many refugees at a more effective pace than any plan that Van could enforce. As the crisis deepened, aid in the form of food, medicines, and building materials began to flow into the camp. This was my area of expertise, and I began to put in eighteen- to twenty-hour days, as much to keep my mind off of my tragic life as to aid the refugees. Tuyen devoted herself to her hospital work, but, try as she might, she could not put the thought of her daughters shortened life out of her mind. One day flowed in to the next, and, as a result of our grief, we grew further and further apart.

Finally, Tuyen came to the realization that since our daughter had been taken from us, we were all each other had, unless we decided to spend our lives immersed in our own grief. Tuyen informed me that I needed to refrain from my relief activities for two days, as she would from her hospital duties, so that we could go away from the encampment so as to communicate our feelings and desires.

She said, "We have known each other for quite some time and sacrificed a great deal in order to be together. We have suffered the ultimate loss of a child and as a result have been forced by circumstances to grow apart. Too much time has passed, and our wounds grow more intense each hour. It is time to confront what has happened and console each other. I still love and respect you. I always will."

"I have spent much time mourning our son and Van's involvement in our tragedy," I told her. "I feel that if we continue to grow apart, we will have lost and become willing participants in his evil life. I continue to love and respect you, and I always will. It is time to put the past away and embrace our future. Our son will always be with us in memory, but it is time to proceed with the rebuilding of our family, in spite of the tragedies that have befallen us."

Tuyen agreed, and we spent the remaining time we had together engulfed in the love we had created in the midst of war. We threw ourselves into the work at hand, never looking back, only looking forward. Our devotion to Buddhism enveloped our lives, and we had a new belief in the future.

Cam Nguyen was in despair. He had grown up on VC island, the son of loving parents and the older brother of Van. Since the VC took over his father's rubber plantation, his hatred of the Communists had dictated his actions. When his father died of a broken heart, Cam enlisted in the Army of the Republic of Vietnam. He went through Officers Candidate School and was quickly exposed to the horrors of war. Although he infrequently saw his mother and brother, he could not help but notice through his mother's comments and his brother's actions that Van had been brainwashed by the Communists. By the time Van was sixteen, he had left home and become a Viet Cong. Cam returned to his village to see if there was anything he could do to save his brother from the Communists.

"When your father died, Van was a lost soul," their mother told him. "He did not see the Viet Cong as enemies of the people but as their saviors."

If Van's father had died as a result of the activities of the Viet Cong, that was too bad. His father had come to represent the Capitalists of the world who were raping Vietnam.

During his final visit home, Cam made an attempt to contact Van and convince him of the error of his ways. They met for the last time close to their home village. They each came alone, Cam unarmed, Van armed to the teeth.

"It is good to see you my brother, even under these circumstances" Cam said.

Van bristled and said, "It grieves me to see you, as you are part and parcel of the Capitalist conspiracy to control Vietnam."

"I am sorry to hear you feel that way," Cam said, "as I love you with all my heart, as does your mother. Do you not see that the Viet Cong and the North Vietnamese are using you as a pawn to control Vietnam in a manner whereby all become subservient to the senior cadre and everyone suffers? It is a form of serfdom refined by Communism to look like salvation, but it is just another form of slavery."

Van replied, "The Communist hierarchy is committed to the freedom and unification of all Vietnam from the Capitalists, from the South Vietnamese lackeys, and in the future from the Chinese and Russians. For hundreds of years, Vietnam has been a colony of one country or another, and the Communists are committed to expelling any and all foreigners from our soil at any cost, no matter how long it takes."

Cam, taken aback by Van's dedication to the cause, replied, "I agree with your sentiments concerning the occupation of Vietnam by outsiders, but you must understand that the Communists do not offer the common man anything but blood, sweat, and tears, and even a victory will only result in slavery. The capitalists offer each individual the opportunity to be as great a human being as possible."

Van responded by firing a burst of his AK-47 over Cam's head. "I reject your statements, and when we are victorious, I will search you out, eliminate your family, and destroy you!"

With that, Van fired again, coming within inches of hitting Cam, and disappeared into the jungle.

Cam returned to his mother in despair, revealing to her the depths of Van's commitment. Taking his leave, he returned to his wife and two children in Saigon, telling them only that he'd had a pleasant visit with his mother.

As the war continued, Cam was heroic in battle and a brilliant strategist, becoming a lieutenant colonel. During the TET offensive, Cam was in charge of the defense of Saigon, early on seeing his troops succumb to the surprise attacks but knowing that the superior force of arms of the Allied forces would turn the tide. He was horrified by the atrocities committed by the Viet Cong and further despondent knowing that his brother, Van, was directing these attacks.

As time went on and Cam realized that the American public no longer supported the war. The writing was on the wall that the South Vietnamese were doomed. Several times he came close to confronting Van in battle, but Van always escaped to Cambodia. As it became apparent that the Allied forces would succumb to the Communists, Cam attempted to have his family escape Vietnam, but they refused to leave without him. After Saigon fell, Cam fought to the bitter end and was captured. Placed in solitary confinement for ninety days, with little food and water, he had no idea what had become of his family.

At the end of ninety days, he was brought out of his dungeon only to be confronted by Van. "It is time to partially fulfill my promise to you of many years ago to destroy you and your family when we became victorious," Van said before having Cam's wife and children brought out. First, he had the children tied to a stake under which sat giant red ant hills. Van himself proceeded to slice bits of skin from the children's bodies, driving the red ants into a frenzy as they lapped up the blood of the children.

Cam and his wife could only look on in horror as their children screamed in agony in their death throes. Next, Van had Cam's wife raped repeatedly by thirty Viet Cong in a very aggressive manner, had her tied to a stake, and made Cam watch as she was consumed by flames. Van laughed hysterically as this tragedy unfolded and said, "This is the price you pay for treason, Cam!"

Placed again in solitary confinement, Cam decided he would appear to be brainwashed by the Communist propaganda, only to destroy Van.

CHAPTER

46

After the horrible deaths of Cam's family, he was taken to an interrogation room. Van directed a nonphysical interrogation. Still being in a state of shock over his horrible murders, Cam was totally unresponsive. Van was not surprised by this fact, having conducted interrogations of such prisoners before. He knew that by treating Cam with kid gloves, his vulnerability to questioning would be enhanced. For thirty days, Cam was exposed to a form of gentle brainwashing, with no effort made to torture him.

Van took over the interrogation personally. "My much beloved brother, I have no intention of destroying you, either mentally or physically. You are the only family I have left. I regret the horrible fate of your family, but it was necessary to show no personal favoritism to my family. I did what I did in order to spare your life. Now we are at a point where we must begin anew, brother to brother. I will try to understand your point of view, and, hopefully, you will try to understand mine. Hopefully we will meet somewhere in the middle."

Cam had no response, only a dead stare.

Van took it upon himself to enunciate his position. "When we were young, I admired and respected our father, mother, and you. When you joined the ARVN and the war progressed, I began to question our loyalty to the Saigon government. After seeing so many innocent people killed by Allied forces, I realized that the only way the Vietnamese people could gain their independence was through victory of the Communists. I spoke about this in detail with our father, and he was adamant about his loyalty to the Saigon government and his hatred of the Communists. Everyone thought that his early passing was the result of the VC takeover of the plantation, but it was really caused by my defection to the VC. I did not and do not mourn him.

"Tuyen and I fell in love at an early age, pledging our lives to each other. She became a spy for the Communists, while I became the pupil of Colonel Khan while rising through the ranks. Tuyen's main source of information was a young intelligence officer named Tom. We met in combat on VC island, Ap Bac, and I employed a suicide bomber to eliminate him, as he became convinced of the preparations for the TET offensive. Unfortunately he was only wounded.

"It became obvious that Tuyen had become more enamored of him as time went on. She also became more repulsed by the means I used to accomplish my goals. When the TET offensive began, Tuyen informed me that Colonel Khan was going to escape to France with her, so I murdered him and Tuyen and I escaped to Cambodia. Tom disappeared, and we assumed he had died during TET. After TET, I was assigned the role of recruiting anyone possible for the VC, as they had been destroyed by the Allies. I used whatever means available—assassinations, torture, kidnapping—to achieve the number of recruits the North Vietnamese required.

"As Tuyen became aware of my methods, she grew emotionally distant from me. When Tom reappeared assigned to the Peace Corps, she fled to his arms and married him, bearing a child. In an attempt to eliminate Tom and Tuyen, her family got in the way and died. The child was eliminated by my terrorist bomb on a refugee flight. I will someday kill Tom and Tuyen as well.

"I am trying to make it clear to you, my brother, that at heart, I am a good man but totally dedicated to the Communist cause, and those who oppose me will be eliminated. You are my only living relative, and I beseech you to look at the fact that I have done whatever necessary to accomplish the goals of Communism yet remain a human being. You will have time to think about what I have said and come to your own conclusions."

Cam could only comprehend part of what Van was saying as he concentrated on the idea that their father's death had been caused by Van's devotion to Communism as much as anything. It would take Cam many days to assimilate the rest of Van's words.

Cam was left unattended with plenty of food, comfortable surroundings, plenty of sleep, no guards, and no further interrogations. In his damaged mind, his life prior to his family's deaths never existed. His life began with Van's declaration of love and request for a reconciliation. Cam's mind and emotions had been purged of his past, and eventually, he looked forward to the future. Van became the center of Cam's universe, as Van visited him every day, further indoctrinating him in the advantages of living under a Communist regime.

One day, Van said, "Our father would have been allowed to oversee the rubber plantation if he had bought in to the precepts of Communism. He was too greedy to do so. The people of South Vietnam would not have been subjected to the horrors of war, nor the atrocities that were necessary for us to be victorious. We would be well on our way to being an independent country, free of outside influence and able to utilize our resources for our own benefit. As it is, we are heavily dependent on the Russians for any economic aid they are willing to give us in the hope that we will become a satellite state adjacent to China. We must stand on our own two feet. Soon, I am quite certain, I will be promoted to General and reside in North Vietnam as the voice of South Vietnam. I hope you will have become as convinced of the honor of our ideology as I and will accompany me as my aide de camp."

Cam heard these words with optimism and slept well for the first time since Saigon fell.

CHAPTER

47

Cam became more and more the psychological slave to Van's wishes. This achieved two things. First, the people Van had to reeducate saw the importance of adhering to Van's protocol and acted accordingly. Secondly, Cam's slavish behavior boosted Van's ego and made him even more of an egomaniac. The brainwashing technique Van used on Cam led him to incorporate this method with the mass of those remaining to be reeducated. People were needed to raise crops, manage the increasing demands of the Communist machine, and maintain the military.

Van continued to receive reports on Tuyen and me, which he stored in his revenge memory bank until his life left room for action. We continued to rebuild our lives, and the organization of the refugee camp continued as aid poured in. I was placed in charge of the distribution of supplies, and Tuyen devoted herself to the development of the hospital operations, giving special attention to the younger patients. Our personal relationship was rooted in the precepts of Buddhism—positive and optimistic.

Soon, Tuyen became pregnant again. Unbeknownst to us, Van's spies were keeping him apprised of our activities. Van's position as head of the reeducation program was almost at an end. He met with Cam and said, "My job here is at an end, with your help. I am being summoned to Hanoi to institute the same program in the North, as there are many there who have to be reeducated. I will be promoted to General, and I wish you to accompany as my Aide De Camp. Together, we will have the opportunity to mold the future of Vietnam."

Cam replied, "My life totally revolves around you. My previous life is a figment of my imagination, serving the mythology of sex and materialism. Thankfully, this part of my life has been removed from my memory and replaced by the glory of your vision. I will follow you anywhere and obey your command."

"I have one mission remaining," Van said, "the elimination of Tom and Tuyen, and I want you to help me."

Cam replied, "Your wish is my command."

They made their way easily to the border of Thailand, where, through bribery and Van's connections in the refugee camp, they were able to determine our daily routine. They waited until after dark to approach our residence, then entered and held us captive.

Van said to Tuyen, "I have known and loved you all my life. You have known from the beginning my dedication to the Communist ideal. You rejected me because I implemented any means to recruit and punish traitors. You fornicated with the enemy and even had a child by him. I saw to it that this child was eliminated, as he was born of a beast. Both of you should have been eliminated, but somehow have not. Now you intend to create another mongoloid child. I cannot allow this."

Van turned to Cam, who carried the AK-47, and said, "Destroy them!"

Cam had not been aware of Tuyen's pregnancy. This brought back his memories of his family and the joy they once experienced. Cam also remembered Van had torturing his family and murdering them. Turning his weapon on Van, Cam pulled the trigger.

Van stared in disbelief, and his final words were, "Tuyen, I will always love you."

55497051R00151

Made in the USA
San Bernardino, CA
02 November 2017